W9-DAN-785

A Bluestocking Guide

Economics

by
Jane A. Williams

based on Richard J. Maybury's book

WHATEVER HAPPENED TO PENNY CANDY?

published by

Bluestocking Press

web site: www.BluestockingPress.com
Phone 800-959-8586

Copyright © 2010 by Jane A. Williams
Previous editions copyrighted 2004, 2000 and 1998

All rights reserved. No part of this book may be used, reproduced, or transmitted in any form or by any means, electronic or mechanical, including photocopying, recording, or by any informational storage or retrieval system, except by a reviewer who may quote brief passages in a review to be printed in a magazine or newspaper, without permission in writing from the author or publisher. Although the author and publisher have researched all sources to ensure the accuracy and completeness of the information contained in this book, we assume no responsibility for errors, inaccuracies, omissions, or any inconsistency herein. Any slights of people or organizations are unintentional.

Printed and bound in the United States of America.
Cover illustration by Bob O'Hara, Georgetown, CA
Cover design by Brian C. Williams, El Dorado, CA

ISBN-13: 978-0-942617-63-4
ISBN-10: 0-942617-63-0

Printed by McNaughton & Gunn, Inc.
Saline, MI USA (January 2013)

Published by
Bluestocking Press • Post Office Box 1014
Placerville, CA 95667-1014 • Phone: 800-959-8586
web site: www.BluestockingPress.com

Quantity Discounts Available

Books published by Bluestocking Press are available at special quantity discounts for bulk purchases to individuals, businesses, schools, libraries, and associations.

For terms and discount schedule contact:

Special Sales Department
Bluestocking Press
Phone: 800-959-8586
email: CustomerService@BluestockingPress.com
web site: www.BluestockingPress.com

Specify the purpose for which the books are being purchased: for gifts, classrooms, fund raisers or premiums — or to be resold.

Contents

Bluestocking Guides are designed to reinforce and enhance a student's understanding of the subject presented in the primer. The subject for this study guide is economics. The primer is WHATEVER HAPPENED TO PENNY CANDY? by Richard J. Maybury.

Given the wide range of age and ability levels of individuals who read WHATEVER HAPPENED TO PENNY CANDY?, it is suggested that students complete the exercises in this study guide that are most age-appropriate or ability-appropriate for them.

Assignment of Exercises

While all given questions and assignments are designed to enhance the student's understanding and retention of the subject matter presented in the primer, it is by no means mandatory that each student complete every exercise in this study guide. This study guide is designed for flexibility based on a student's age, as well as a student's interest in the material presented.

It is strongly suggested that each student complete the Comprehension Exercises, but instructors can preview and then select the Application Exercises, Films to View, and Suggested Books to Read that they wish the student to complete, based on: course time available, student's interest, and/or student's age (some films/books might not be age appropriate — the student might be too young, too old, or the content too advanced for a younger student). Also, depending on the age and interest level of a student, one student might spend weeks on a research assignment, whereas another student might spend a few hours or days.

Suggested Time Frame For Study

This study guide is organized to allow the instructor flexibility in designing the ideal course of study. Therefore, there is no "right" or "wrong" time frame for covering the material; the instructor should tailor the study of the primer and study guide to the student's unique school schedule, learning style, and age. For example, younger students may only complete comprehension exercises, whereas older students may complete additional application exercises, suggested readings, and films.

An easy-to-apply rule of thumb for determining length of study is to divide the number of chapters in a primer by the number of weeks the instructor plans to study the subject/book.

Ideally, the student should read a chapter from the primer and then immediately answer the corresponding questions in the study guide. Chapter length varies, so sometimes a student may be able to read more than one chapter and complete the corresponding questions/exercises in a day. Some instructors may choose to complete the primer in a few short weeks in which case multiple chapters per day will need to be covered. Others may plan to study the primer over an entire semester, so only a few chapters per week will be assigned. The key is to move quickly enough that the student is engaged with learning and also able to absorb all concepts fully. The student's performance on end-of-chapter Questions and Assignments should be a good indication of this.

The time frame for completing application exercises (Discussion/Essay/Assignment/Research) is also subject to the instructor's discretion. Most discussions can take place immediately after reading the chapter. However, students may need a day or two to complete an essay, and some assignments will take outside research requiring additional time. It is best for the instructor to preview the application exercises (Discussion/Essay/Assignment/Research) and assign the student a "due date" based upon the student's cognitive abilities and available course schedule.

Comprehension Exercises

Comprehension Exercises test the degree to which the student understands and retains the information presented in each chapter. In this study guide Comprehension Exercises include: 1) Define, 2) True/False, and 3) Short Answer/Fill-In. Students are encouraged to answer all exercises in complete sentences. The information needed to complete these exercises can usually be found in the given chapter of the primer. Answers will be found in the answer section of this Study Guide.

Define

The student should define the given term based on Richard Maybury's definition provided in the given chapter or glossary (*not* a standard dictionary definition). This is essential. As Richard Maybury says, "Fuzzy language causes fuzzy thinking." For any discussion or explanation to be clearly understood, one must first understand the intended definition of words as used by the author. Confusion and disagreement can occur because the student does not understand the author's intended definition of a word. To reinforce this point, have a student look up the word "law" in an unabridged Webster's dictionary. The student should find a number of definitions following the word "law." Again, unless one agrees on the definition intended for the discussion or study at hand, misunderstanding or "fuzzy thinking" can result.

True/False

For True/False exercises, if the student believes the statement is correct, the student should simply write "True" as the answer. If the student believes the statement is *not* true, the student should write "False." If the student answers the question "False," the student should be sure to state why the statement is *not* true or rewrite the false statement to make it true. In the answer section of this study guide, statements that are "False" are so noted and have been rewritten to make them true.

Short Answer/Fill In

The student should answer Short Answer/Fill In questions based upon knowledge gained from studying the given chapter. Unless the student is asked to use his/her own opinion or knowledge, the answer should be based upon Richard Maybury's statements. Generally, Short Answer/Fill In Questions are selected verbatim from the given chapter.

Application Exercises

With few exceptions, Application Exercises ask the student to apply the knowledge and ideas he/she has gained from a given chapter to "real world" situations. In many cases, these assignments are designed to help the student personalize the information just learned so that the student can better retain and apply the knowledge. In this study guide application exercises include: 1) Discussion, 2) Essay, 3) Assignment, and 4) For Further Research. In the majority of instances, answers to Application Exercises will vary based upon the student's own experiences. Application Exercises are designed to encourage informal discussions among students and instructors, and/or to stimulate students to critically evaluate the scenario. However, the instructor may ask the student to write answers (in essay format, outline, etc.) if a more formal/structure approach is desired.

For Further Reading or To View

The books and films mentioned in For Further Reading and To View are designed to expand students' understanding of concepts presented in the related chapter. No written or verbal reports on the books/movies are usually required, however, students and instructors are encouraged to discuss the ideas presented. Thus, Suggestions for Further Reading/Viewing usually have no set answers and, therefore, may not appear in the "Answer" section. (The instructor may choose to assign a book/movie report of his/her own construction if he/she desires.)

How to Grade Assignments

Define, True/False, Short Answer/Fill-In

To determine the percentage of correct answers, divide the total number of correct answers by the total number of questions. If, for example, a chapter section has two Define questions, one True/False question, and seven Short Answer/Fill-In questions, and the student has answered correctly eight of these questions, the student will have answered 80% of the questions correctly.

$$8 \div 10 = .80 \text{ (or 80\%)}$$

Number of Correct Answers ÷ Number of Total Questions = Percentage of Questions Answered Correctly

In "Grade" equivalents, percentage scores generally range as follows:

90 - 100%	=	A
80 - 89.9%	=	B
70 - 79.9%	=	C
60 - 69.9%	=	D
less than 60%	=	F

In general, a student earning an "A" has demonstrated excellent understanding of the subject matter; a student earning a "B" has demonstrated good understanding of the subject matter; a student earning a "C" has demonstrated sufficient understanding of the subject matter; and a student earning a "D" or "F" would benefit from reviewing the subject matter to strengthen his/her understanding of the topic at hand.

In determining whether a student has provided a "right" or "wrong" answer to a question, the instructor should compare the student's answers with the answers provided in this guide. True/False, Fill-In, and Define questions/answers are straightforward. Short Answer questions/answers are also generally straightforward; on some longer answers the student's wording may vary slightly from the answer provided in this study guide, but the student should receive full credit if the *content* of his/her answer is correct. When in doubt, it is recommended that the instructor refer back to the chapter in the primary text to reference what the author said about the issue at hand.

"Answers Will Vary"

In the answer section of this study guide you will sometimes come across an answer that reads "answers will vary" for a given question. This generally means that the student is required to answer the question using his/her own knowledge, experience, or intuition. In these instances, the instructor should refer back to the chapter in the primary text to reference what the author said about the issue at hand compared to the student's answer; a "correct" answer should be thoughtful, complete, and on-topic.

Discussion/Essay/Assignment

These assignments are provided so that students can apply the concepts they learned in the given chapter to their own experiences, current events, or historical events—to make the concepts more meaningful. In most cases, it is extremely difficult to "grade" the completed assignments as "right" or "wrong." Instead, the instructor should provide guidance for these assignments. The completeness, thoughtfulness, enthusiasm, and meaning the student brings to the assignment will serve as an indication of the student's mastery of the assignment. If the instructor then wishes to assign a grade, he/she may elect to do so. Or, these assignments may be non-graded "extra credit," serving to boost the student's overall grade for the course.

Author's Disclosure and Point of View

Short Answer/Fill-In/True or False

1. What is Juris Naturalism?

Discussion/Essay/Assignment

2. In the "Author's Disclosure" Richard Maybury says that few writers disclose the viewpoints or opinions they use to decide what information is important and what is not, or what data will be presented and what data omitted. Collect several history books from your home library, school library, or public library. Do the authors of the books you collected disclose their viewpoints or opinions to the reader? Do the authors disclose what criteria they used to determine what information or data to include in the book and what to omit? Explain why it is, or is not, important to have biases disclosed. What benefit, if any, does a reader or viewer have (in the case of movies, televised news, or documentaries) if he or she is able to determine the viewpoint of a writer?

3. Richard Maybury (Uncle Eric) believes that all history is slanted based on the facts historians choose to report. Can you provide examples of material you have read or to which you have listened where facts have been reported but perhaps not all the facts? If no books come to mind, have you had arguments or disagreements between siblings or friends in which, when asked, each person presented his/her side of the argument—presenting only those facts that best favored his/her side of the story? How can you learn to identify the slants of writers, news commentators, friends, etc.?

4. Read the quotes in the "Author's Disclosure" section of this book that help to describe the Juris Naturalist viewpoint. Look up the definition of "unalienable" in a current dictionary. Compare a current dictionary's definition with the definition from NOAH WEBSTER's 1828 DICTIONARY: "Unalienable; that cannot be legally or justly alienated or transferred to another ... All men have certain natural rights which are 'inalienable'."

5. Samuel Adams defined the natural rights of the colonists as the right to life, liberty, and property. Why do you think "property" was changed to "happiness" in the Declaration of Independence? *(Optional exercise: You can turn this into a research exercise by researching primary source documents of America's Founders to see if you can find the answer for the change from "property" to "happiness." Provide support for your position.)*

6. Select one of the quotes from the "Author's Disclosure" section of this book and write a short essay about what the quote means to you.

For Further Reading

7. Read HOW TO LIE WITH STATISTICS by Darrell Huff, published by W.W. Norton. Its purpose is to warn its readers to be on the lookout for the misleading use of statistics. It shows how statistics can be used to distort truth. A modern classic, excellent book. For ages 14 and up.

8. Read EVALUATING BOOKS: WHAT WOULD THOMAS JEFFERSON THINK ABOUT THIS? an Uncle Eric book by Richard J. Maybury. This book provides key indicators and terms to help the reader learn how to identify the slants of authors, media commentators, and others. Published by Bluestocking Press, web site: www.BluestockingPress.com. For ages 13 and up.

9. Visit the following online sites with parental oversight and guidance: 1) *The Daily Bell* at www.thedailybell.com describes itself as "the only periodical that analyzes power-elite dominant social themes from a free market perspective." On a daily basis, mainstream articles are reprinted in part or in whole and analyzed/commented on from the *The Daily Bell's* free market perspective. As you study WHATEVER HAPPENED TO PENNY CANDY, read as many of their daily posts (that are content and age appropriate) as possible, so you learn to identify the philosophical viewpoints of the authors of news and editorial articles: i.e., Centrist, Libertarian, Liberal, Conservative, Independent. For help with this exercise, if a student has limited knowledge of political and economic bias, the student should first read Richard J. Maybury's book ARE YOU LIBERAL? CONSERVATIVE? OR CONFUSED? published by Bluestocking Press, or wait to do this exercise until that book is read. 2) A more advanced assignment is to visit www.worldpress.org which includes "news and views from around the world". Are you able to identify the philosophical slants of the varied authors of these articles?

Thought Questions

Before you begin to read WHATEVER HAPPENED TO PENNY CANDY? answer the following three questions and provide support based on your current knowledge and/or opinions. Save your response. You will revisit these questions at a later time.

1. Write an essay explaining what you currently know about economics. Also answer the following question: How important is economics in a person's everyday life?

2. What do you think is the root cause of America's economic problems?

3. In the course of one day, how often do you discuss economics or seek out news regarding the economy?

A Suggestion to Teachers

from

Richard J. Maybury

If you are teaching individuals who have had little exposure to the "real world" of money and business, the individual's understanding of WHATEVER HAPPENED TO PENNY CANDY? will be aided by briefly covering the following concepts before reading the book. It is not essential to cover these concepts, but it is helpful.

1. The law of supply and demand.

   a. If supply decreases or demand increases, the price tends to rise, other things being equal.

   b. If supply increases or demand decreases, the price tends to fall, other things being equal.

2. Specialization of labor.

3. Wealth is not money. Wealth is the goods and services people produce. Money is the tool we use to trade wealth.

4. The economy is the system of producing and distributing wealth.

5. Government is financed by taxes.

6. It is production, not work, that is important. Work is merely wasted effort unless something of value is produced.

7. We cannot consume more than we produce.

Brief articles follow which provide excellent introductions to economic principles. Suggested age levels are listed for each article.

For further study, the bibliography listed at the conclusion of this study guide contains some excellent sources of information which are interesting, clearly written, and explain the above concepts in detail.

—Richard J. Maybury

Before you begin to read
WHATEVER HAPPENED TO PENNY CANDY?

Pages 12-38 include several short articles which provide excellent introductions to economic principles. It is suggested that students read those articles that are most age appropriate before beginning the book WHATEVER HAPPENED TO PENNY CANDY? Suggested age levels are listed after each title, and are to be used as a general guideline only (see boxed listing at the bottom of this page). Teachers should review the articles, then assess the student's reading and comprehension ability to determine which article/s a student is ready to tackle. Three major articles are reprinted, each discussing general economic concepts. Following each major article are related articles which reinforce concepts discussed in the major articles.

Articles recommended "for parents, teachers and others" were originally written for parents or teachers to help them learn how to introduce economic principles to the very young. However, any student who is capable of comprehending the articles should read them.

Before students begin to read the articles, ask them to answer the following two questions:

What is economics?
Why is it important to study economics?

(Note: These two questions are designed to determine what information or misinformation, if any, students have about this topic, prior to their reading WHATEVER HAPPENED TO PENNY CANDY? Answers will vary. A written response is preferred since these answers should be saved and the questions asked again at the completion of their course of study. Compare pre- and post- answers at that time.)

Ask students to identify examples or explanations of the concepts listed in *A Suggestion to Teachers* (#1-7 on page 10). Have students place the number of the concept (i.e. #1 represents the law of supply and demand) in the margin of the article next to the section where, for example, the law of supply and demand is explained, or an example given. (i.e. see example in *Free Market: Elementary, My Child* that begins on page 37).

Besides those articles reprinted in this study guide, it is highly recommended that you borrow or purchase the following book. It will be referred to often in this study guide and is available for purchase through its publisher, Bluestocking Press (www.BluestockingPress.com).

ECONOMICS: A FREE MARKET READER, published by Bluestocking Press (phone: 800-959-8586, web site: www.BluestockingPress.com). For ages 13 and up.

Other resources that are referred to in this study guide are also listed in the bibliography and resource sections of this study guide.

Page #	Major Article (age level)	Page #	Related Articles (age level)
12	1. Economics for Boys and Girls (for parents, teachers, & ages 12 and up)	15	Letter to His Stepbrother (for ages 12 and up)
16	2. The Wondrous Toy Store (for ages 14 and up)	20	I, Pencil (for ages 14 and up)
		24	Letter to His Grandson (for ages 12 and up)
		26	The Cow in the Apartment (for ages 12 and up)
28	3. Start at the Beginning (for ages 14 and up)	32	Why Pay for Things? (for parents, teachers, & ages 10 and up)
		34	Ownership Responsibility and the Child (for ages 15 and up)

1. Economics for Boys and Girls
by Leonard E. Read
(for parents, teachers, and others ages 12 up)

Time and again we have been asked to devise economic instruction for the youngsters, the thought being that it's the oncoming generation that counts. And, just as often, we have shaken our heads, pleading ignorance of how to go about it.

Trying to devise economic lessons for grown-ups has seemed difficult enough, for only now and then is there an adult who shows any interest in or aptitude for the subject. But we have tried, and over the years of trial and error, it has seemed that our best approach to adults is to leave them alone until they seek such instruction or light as we may come to possess. In other words, our job, as we now see it, is to concentrate on improving our own understanding and practice of freedom, with faith that others will be attracted precisely to the extent that we are able to show self-improvement.

Thus, we are constantly striving to better understand and explain and apply the economics of specialization and the division of labor, freedom in transactions, the marginal utility theory of value, and reliance on the orderliness of the free market as a guide to creativities and exchange.

Is there a way to present such complex ideas to children so that they might be attracted toward the free market way of social behavior? Perhaps. But first, let us consider our raw material, the youngsters we would teach.

There are those who contend that every baby starts life as a little savage; that he is equipped, among other things, with organs and muscles over which he has no control, with an urge for self-preservation, with aggressive drives and emotions like anger, fear, and love over which he likewise has practically no control, and that in the process

of growing up, it is normal for every child to be dirty, to fight, to talk back, to disobey, to evade. *"Every child has to grow out of delinquent behavior."* So runs this argument. For my part, however, I take small comfort in this Freudian view of the genesis of the human race. I would much prefer to think of the child as a budding plant with all the potential for beauty and happiness which such a growing organism portends. In each case, of course, there may be from the adult point of view, apparent disorganization, lack of coordination, and disharmony. Yet, the potential for harmony and beauty is there.

Whether the child be considered a brutal barbarian or a budding beauty, the challenge is to help him emerge from a state of ignorance as to his relationship with others and into harmony with the universal laws which govern the human situation. The child is an extension of the parent's responsibility, and that responsibility includes pointing the child in the direction of sound economic understanding. I shall hint at, but by no means exhaust, the possibilities:

If you open a door, close it.

This is a sequel to the above; it is merely another practice that conforms the wisdom of completing each of life's transactions.

An inevitable dualism bisects nature, so that each thing is a half, and suggests another thing to make it whole; as spirit, matter; man, woman; subjective, objective; in, out; upper, under; motion, rest; yea, nay.[1]

For child training, I would add: drop, pick up; open, close; and others.

If you make a promise, keep it.

Social chaos has no better ally than broken promises. Children not brought up to keep their word will be the authors of treaties written not to be observed; they'll run for office on bogus platforms, cancel gold contracts, use the political means to expropriate property; they'll sell their souls to gain fame or fortune or power. Not only will they fail to be honest with their fellow men; they will not even heed the dictates of their own conscience. On the other hand, children brought up to keep their promises will not go back on their bond...Integrity will be their mark of distinction!

Whatever you borrow, pay back.

This is an extension of promise keeping. An adherence to these admonitions develops a respect for private property, a major premise in sound economic doctrine. No person, thus brought up, would think of feathering his own nest at the expense of others. Welfare statists and social planners are not born of this training, that is, if the training really sinks in. True, a socialist will honor debts incurred in his own name but will disregard any indebtedness he sponsors in the name of "the public." He has not been brought up to understand that the principle of compensation applies "across the board."

Play the thank-you game.

It will take a brilliant parent and a mighty perceptive child to get anywhere with this one. I can set forth the idea but not how to teach it. The idea, once grasped, is simple enough, yet so evasive that...it was only discovered a bare century ago: The value of a good or service is determined not *objectively* by cost of production, *but subjectively* by what others will give in willing exchange. Economic science has no more important concept than this; the free market has no other economic genesis than this subjective or marginal utility theory of value. Indeed, it is most accurately identified as the free market theory of value.

To repeat an illustration used earlier: When mother exchanges 30¢ for a can of beans, she values the beans more than the 30¢ and the grocer values the 30¢ more than the beans. If mother valued the 30¢ more than the beans, she wouldn't trade. If the grocer valued his beans more than the 30¢, he wouldn't trade. The value of both the 30¢ and the beans (excluding other considerations) is determined by the two subjective judgments. The amount of effort exerted (cost) to obtain the 30¢ or to acquire the beans has nothing to do with the value of either the beans or the 30¢.

I repeat, the value of any good or service is determined by what it will bring in willing, *not forcible* or unwilling, exchange.[2] When the 30¢ is exchanged for the beans, the grocer concludes the transaction with "Thank you," for, in his judgment, he has gained. There is precisely the same justification for the mother to say, "Thank you," for, in her judgment, she has gained. It wouldn't be at all amiss to describe this as "the thank-you way of economic life."

This concept of value, be it remembered, was practiced off and on by the common man ages before economic theorists identified it as the efficacious way of mutually advancing economic well-being. And, by the same token, the child can be taught to practice it before he can possibly grasp the theory. In exchanging toys or marbles or jacks or whatever with another, can he not play the thank-you game? Can he not be taught to express the same "thank you" himself as he expects from his playmate? That something is wrong with the trade if this is not the case? That both have gained when each says, "Thank you"? Accomplish this with a boy or girl and you have laid the groundwork for sound economic thinking.

Do nothing to a playmate you wouldn't enjoy having him do to you.

Moral philosophy is the investigation into and the study of what's right and wrong. Economics is a division of this discipline: the study of right and wrong in economic affairs.

The free market is the Golden Rule in its economic application, thus free market economics is dependent on the practice of the Golden Rule.

That the Golden Rule can be phrased and taught so as to be completely perceived prior to adolescence is doubtful. Its apprehension requires a moral nature, a faculty rarely acquired earlier than teenage—in many instances, never!

But the effort to teach the Golden Rule to boys and girls will, at a minimum, result in a better observation of it on the parent's part. Children highly impressionable—are far more guided by parental conduct than by parental admonishments. Thus, the attempt to teach this fundamental principle of morality and justice, *resulting in highly exemplary behavior,* may lead the child first to imitation and then to habitual observance and practice.

---

[1] Excerpted from *Compensation* by Ralph Waldo Emerson.

[2] TVA, Post Office, and a thousand and one other deficits, are paid for by forcible exchange. Moon specialists are paid by forcible, not willing, exchange. This goes, also, for all governmental subsidies.

Condensed and reprinted with permission of the Foundation for Economic Education, 30 S. Broadway, Irvington-on-Hudson, New York 10533, web address: http://fee.org

---

Note: For further reading in regards to *Whatever you borrow, pay back* in the above article read *Letter to His Stepbrother* (for ages 12 and up) that begins on the next page.

Letter to His Stepbrother
by Abraham Lincoln
(for ages 12 and up)

Pioneer life was hard for a man with two children but no woman to care for them, nor to help with the chores at home. Thus Thomas Lincoln remarried about a year after the death (1818) of his first wife, Nancy Hanks, Abraham's mother. The new "mother" was a widow, Sarah Bush Johnston, with three youngsters of her own. According to historians, Abraham Lincoln's stepbrother, John D. Johnston, five years Lincoln's junior, turned out to be shiftless and lazy. The following letter (reproduced from the original manuscript with slight changes only in style and form) was written to his young stepbrother when Lincoln was 39 years old and a U.S. Congressman from Illinois.

Washington
December 24, 1848

Dear Johnston:

Your request for eighty dollars I do not think it best to comply with now. At the various times when I have helped you a little, you have said to me, "We can get along very well now," but in a very short time I find you in the same difficulty again. Now this can only happen by some defect in your conduct. What that defect is, I think I know. You are not lazy, and still you are an idler. I doubt whether since I saw you, you have done a good whole day's work, in any one day. You do not very much dislike to work; and still you do not work too much, merely because it does not seem to you that you could get much for it. This habit of needlessly wasting time, is the whole difficulty; and it is vastly important to you, and still more so to your children, that you should break this habit. It is more important to them, because they have longer to live, and can keep out of an idle habit before they are in it, easier than they can get out after they are in.

You are now in need of some money; and what I propose is, that you shall go to work, "tooth and nails," for somebody who will give you money for it. Let father and your boys take charge of things at home—prepare for a crop, and make the crop; and you go to work for the best money wages, or in discharge of any debt you owe, that you can get. And to secure you a fair reward for your labor, I now promise you that for every dollar you will, between this and the first of next May, get for your own labor, either in money, or on your own indebtedness, I will then give you one other dollar. By this, if you hire yourself at ten dollars a month, from me you will get ten more, making twenty dollars a month for your work. In this, I do not mean you shall go off to St. Louis, or the lead mines, or the gold mines in California, but I [mean for you to go at it for the best wages you] can get close to home in Coles County. Now if you will do this, you will be soon out of debt, and what is better, you will have a habit that will keep you from getting in debt again. But if I should now clear you out, next year you would be just as deep in as ever. You say you would almost give your place in Heaven for $70 or $80. Then you value your place in Heaven very cheaply, for I am sure you can with the offer I make you get the seventy or eighty dollars for four or five months work. You say if I furnish you the money you will deed me the land, and, if you don't pay the money back, you will deliver possession. Nonsense! If you can't now live with the land, how will you then live without it? You have always been [kind] to me, and I do not now mean to be unkind to you. On the contrary, if you will but follow my advice, you will find it worth more than eight times eighty dollars to you.

Affectionately your brother,
A. Lincoln

Reprinted with permission of the Economic Education, 30 S. Broadway, Irvington-on-Hudson, New York 10533, web address: http://fee.org

2. The Wondrous Toy Store
or
Why Study Economics?
by
Bettina Bien Greaves
(for ages 14 up)

Toy stores throughout the year are crammed from floor to ceiling with dolls, bicycles, trains, robots, wooden trucks, story books, whatever a child might want. How does it happen that so many toys are collected in one spot for the delight of parents and children? Where do the toys come from? Who thought to produce them, to ship them and to stock them in stores for sale to customers? Did some master planner organize the entire operation from start to finish?

The provisioning of groceries, hardware, and department stores seems just as miraculous. There are big supermarkets, small corner delicatessens, and speciality shops that offer everything from buttons to pencils, from soup to nuts, from clothing to automobiles. We can usually find almost anything we want on the shelves of some store, neatly arranged, just waiting for customers to come in and buy. How does it happen? Did someone conceive of the idea of retail stores and then plan the whole process from scratch—producing raw materials (metals, wood, cloth, plastics, glass, electronics, paper, and so on), transporting them, manufacturing finished items, and then establishing stores all across the land to sell the final products —toys, food, clothing and other items, big and small?

Central Planning Inconceivable

It is inconceivable that a single person, or a group of persons, even with the smartest advisers and the most powerful computers, could plan the whole process of production from beginning to end. No one could possibly organize all the raw material producers, manufacturers, truckers, and merchants needed to carry out such a complex operation. No human being could assure consumers that they would find in the stores the vast array of things they want, in the qualities desired and in sufficient quantities, neither too many nor too few. So how is it done? How is production organized? To answer that question, we must study how men act and how they cooperate. That means we must study economics.

Actions of Individuals

Each of us is a unique individual. Everyone has his or her own wants, values, preferences, goals. Each of us has his or her own special talents, aptitudes, interests. Each of us can, of course, accomplish some things by ourselves, but because of our personal shortcomings we can't do very much when we work alone. None of us is strong or clever enough to produce everything he or she wants. It usually takes hard work and effort to transform natural resources into things we can eat, wear, and use. We get tired after we work for a while. We also lack the means, the resources and the tools, to do everything alone. Fortunately, we don't have to be self-sufficient; we can, and do cooperate with others.

Everyone of us has many wants, some more important to us than others. Everyone of us acts in the attempt to attain our most urgent goals as best we can given our interests and abilities. But there is a limit to what we can accomplish by ourselves.

Interpersonal Cooperation

One of the fundamental facts of life is that an individual can accomplish more by cooperating, by working with other people, than he or she can by working alone. Through cooperation, a person has the opportunity to attain more complex and more far-reaching goals than he or she could ever hope to accomplish alone. These actions and interactions of individuals are what economists study. The economist analyzes the separate actions of individuals, their consequences, and their impact on others. The economist also studies the cooperative efforts of individuals and the way such activities affect others. Thus economics helps us understand the advantages of peaceful and voluntary cooperation among men.

History reveals who, what, where, and when; history describes the changes men have wrought. Psychology, philosophy, religion explain *why*. Economics tells us *how*.

Long ago, in prehistoric times, men used to live in small groups or tribes. Everyone shared work and responsibilities according to age and ability. Soon they began to specialize and to cooperate in order to accomplish things they couldn't do alone. Every individual, even in a small primitive community, has a somewhat different assortment of wants, goals, values, preferences, and ideas. Thus, in time they discovered that the easiest way to obtain some goods and services was by offering to barter with others the product of their own specialized labor, clay pots for woven blankets, for instance, or a fishing net for an axe. By trading what they produced for the production of others, both parties to a trade gained something they valued more than the item they gave in trade. Otherwise they wouldn't trade.

Helping Oneself by Producing for Others

Years later, when economists began to study the actions of men and fully recognized the advantages of trade, they pointed out that we help ourselves by producing for others. If we are in business for ourselves, we must offer a good or service others want, or go out of business. And when we take a job working for someone else, we are also producing for others; we are helping our employer accomplish what he or she wants; in exchange we receive wages or a salary which help us accomplish something we want, pay for food and lodging, make some special purchase, or save for college.

By studying how exchanges develop, how individuals accomplish their own personal goals by producing and then trading with others, economists came to understand the origin of complex markets, large-scale wide-ranging transactions and even today's fully-stocked specialized retail stores. This understanding of markets explained how natural resources are developed, transformed into finished products, and transported to the retail stores for consumers to buy. This understanding explains the wondrous toy store.

Producing Bicycles

Let's take an example, bicycles. What are bicycles made of? The frame is made of special alloy steel tubing, held together by a steel or brass alloy. Chain, axle, rivets, the rim and the spokes of the wheels are also all made of certain kinds of steel. The crank is made of heat-treated aluminum alloy. All moving parts rest on ball bearings. A bicycle has rubber-pad brakes. Its pneumatic tires are made of real or synthetic rubber (butyl) and a tough fabric, cotton, nylon, or silk. An adhesive is used to attach the outer tire cover to the inner tube of racing bikes. Bicycle saddles are made of leather, rubber or plastic. The bike may have a wire basket carrier or carrier bags of leather or canvas and perhaps a lamp powered by battery or dynamo. Now where do all the materials used to produce bicycles come from? steel, brass, and aluminum alloys? real rubber? synthetic rubber? ball bearings? cotton? nylon? silk? adhesive? leather? canvas? plastic? dry cell batteries or dynamos?

Many persons are involved in helping to find and extract the minerals, grow and harvest the rubber, cotton, and silk. Many others save and invest in order to build plants or factories where these raw materials can be processed. Still other persons help to produce the trucks, trains, ships and planes to transport them from iron mine, rubber or cotton plantation, silk farm, cattle ranch. Others work to build processing plants and factories. Only when the iron has been turned into steel tubing, rugged steel rivets, bicycle wheel rims and spokes, only when the rubber has been converted into bicycle tires and bicycle saddles, only when all the parts are manufactured, can they be assembled in a bicycle factory into bicycles.

The individuals involved in this complex process of production, manufacture and assembly of bicycles were not producing for themselves. Each was exchanging something he had—time, effort, and labor—for something he preferred—money with which to buy the goods and services needed to live and enjoy life. Thus each was producing for others. Yet at the same time, he or she was helping him—or herself by engaging in a gigantic cooperative effort that ranged from the mine and rubber plantation to the final consumer—people young and old who ride bikes for work, and cyclists who race in competition.

Entrepreneurs

Every stage in the gigantic cooperative process of production begins with an idea. The men and women whose ideas help to improve and coordinate production are known as "entrepreneurs." Entrepreneurs are responsible for thinking up ways to supply consumers with bicycles, as well as toys, automobiles, dry goods, computers, TVs,

hardware, fresh fruits, vegetables, and every other conceivable item we find in our stores today.

An entrepreneur looks for an opportunity to supply consumers with a good or service they will want, at a price they will be willing to pay. Or to supply producers with something that will contribute to further production. He searches for clues in people's purchases and activities. He considers the prices currently being asked and paid for the factors he needs for production. He looks at the prices consumers are now offering and paying for similar products. He then calculates costs of raw materials, transportation, labor, manufacturing, advertising, retailing, and so on.

An entrepreneur is lured by the hope of profiting if he succeeds. If he believes his idea will result in a new, better, or cheaper product, or a product that is both better and cheaper than what is now on the market, he will undertake the project. If he succeeds in producing a product for less than consumers are willing to pay, he will have channeled new materials and/or unfinished factors of production that were undervalued, into goods and services that have a greater value. His profit will consist of the difference between the value of the factors of production in their earlier use and their value in his new product. On the other hand, if his selling prices do not cover costs, he will suffer a loss; he will have wasted raw materials that would have been more valuable to consumers in another use. The unsuccessful entrepreneur will have to change his ways or go out of business. Thus, market prices guide entrepreneurs, while profits or losses give them direction and keep them from wasting scarce resources.

Entrepreneurs coordinate the various stages of production from the mines and farms to the final consumer. They are guided by prices, by the lure of profit, and they are made cautious by the fear of loss. It is they who provide opportunities to individual workers to accomplish their respective goals most easily and effectively by cooperating, producing for others, and trading the results of their efforts.

In the eyes of economics, the market is a complicated process, far too complex for any master planner to organize. The market is always changing and evolving, as countless individuals — entrepreneurs, workers, traders, buyers, sellers — cooperate, interact, adopt new ideas and adjust to new conditions. It is through their effort and initiative that grocery stores are stocked with food, clothing stores with suits and dresses, hardware stores with tools, automobile sales rooms with autos, minivans and jeeps, appliance stores with refrigerators, stoves, radios, TVs, computers, and so on.

Economics: A Guide to A Peaceful Society

We live in a complex world. It is not always easy to remember that the best way to accomplish our own goals is to produce for others through the market. Economics reminds us by explaining how the market functions. Economics explains why entrepreneurs should be free to experiment, to search, to discover opportunities, and to undertake new ventures. It explains how savers and investors contribute by providing producers with tools and machines. It explains the advantages of social cooperation. Thus it fosters friendly interpersonal relations. It also helps to bring people together all over the world and so reduces the chance of friction or conflict.

Economics also offers a guide to government policy. It explains the importance of protecting life and property. It shows us how to recognize programs that hamper entrepreneurs, frustrate savers and investors, and make production more difficult and expensive. It enables us to distinguish between policies that permit people to accomplish their various ends by peaceful and moral means and those policies that hamper them.

If we learn the lesson economics teaches, entrepreneurs will be free to undertake new ventures without outside interference, savers will be rewarded and shops will be well stocked with things consumers want — toys, food, automobiles, computers, telephones, and so on. But more than that, each of us will be free to pursue our various goals; peaceful and voluntary transactions will proceed relatively smoothly and society will flourish.

Bettina Bien Greaves, an economist, was a long-time staff member, resident scholar, and trustee of The Foundation for Economic Education, Inc., (Irvington-on-Hudson, New York 10533). She studied for many years with Ludwig von Mises, the dean of the Austrian (free market) School of Economics.

Note: For further reading on the concept *Helping Oneself by Producing for Others* (explained in *The Wondrous Toy Store*) read the following three articles: *I, Pencil* (page 20); *Letter to His Grandson* (page 24); and *The Cow in the Apartment* (page 26). Each is reprinted with permission of the Foundation for Economic Education, 30 S. Broadway, Irvington-on-Hudson, New York 10533, web address: http://fee.org

I, Pencil
by Leonard E. Read
(for ages 12 and up)

To summarize the philosophy of freedom and marvel at the results, one must wonder at the mystery of the creation of so simple an item as a lead pencil.

Here is a pencil's story as told to Leonard Read in 1958. The pencil's official name is "Mongol 482." Its many ingredients are assembled, fabricated, and finished in Eberhard Faber Pencil Company, Wilkes-Barre, Pennsylvania.

I am a lead pencil—the ordinary wooden pencil familiar to all boys and girls and adults who can read and write. Writing is both my vocation and my avocation; that's all I do.

You may wonder why I should write a genealogy. Well, to begin with, my story is interesting. And, next, I am a mystery—more so than a tree or a sunset or even a flash of lightning. But, sadly, I am taken for granted by those who use me, as if I were a mere incident and without background. This supercilious attitude relegates me to the level of the commonplace. This is a species of the grievous error in which mankind cannot too long persist without peril. For, the wise G. K. Chesterton observed, "We are perishing for want of wonder, not for want of wonders."

I, Pencil, simple though I appear to be, merit your wonder and awe, a claim I shall attempt to prove. In fact, if you can understand me—no, that's too much to ask of anyone—if you can become aware of the miraculousness which I symbolize, you can help save the freedom mankind is so unhappily losing. I have a profound lesson to teach. And I can teach this lesson better than can an automobile or an airplane or a mechanical dishwasher because—well, because I am seemingly so simple.

Simple? Yet, *not a single person on the face of this earth knows how to make me*. This sounds fantastic, doesn't it? Especially when it is realized that there are about one and one-half billion of my kind produced in the U.S.A. each year.

Pick me up and look me over. What do you see? Not much meets the eye—there's some wood, lacquer, the printed labeling, graphite lead, a bit of metal, and an eraser.

Innumerable Antecedents

Just as you cannot trace your family tree back very far, so is it impossible for me to name and explain all my antecedents. But I would like to suggest enough of them to impress upon you the richness and complexity of my background.

My family tree begins with what in fact is a tree, a cedar of straight grain that grows in Northern California and Oregon. Now contemplate all the saws and trucks and rope and the countless other gear used in harvesting and carting the cedar logs to the railroad siding. Think of all the persons and the numberless skills that went into their fabrication: the mining of ore, the making of steel and its refinement into saws, axes, motors; the growing of hemp and bringing it through all the stages to heavy and strong rope; the logging camps with their beds and mess halls, the cookery and the raising of all the foods. Why, untold thousands of persons had a hand in every cup of coffee the loggers drink!

The logs are shipped to a mill in San Leandro, California. Can you imagine the individuals who make flat cars and rails and railroad engines and who construct and install the communication systems incidental thereto? These legions are among my antecedents.

Consider the millwork in San Leandro. The cedar logs are cut into small, pencil-length slats less than one-fourth of an inch in thickness. These are kiln dried and then tinted for the same reason women put rouge on their faces. People prefer that I look pretty, not a pallid white. The slats are waxed and kiln dried again. How many skills went into the making of the tint and the kilns, into supplying the heat, the light and power, the belts, motors, and all the other things a mill requires? Sweepers in the mill among my ancestors? Yes, and included are the men who poured the concrete for the dam of a Pacific Gas & Electric Company hydroplant which supplies the mill's power!

Don't overlook the ancestors present and distant who have a hand in transporting sixty car-loads of slats across the nation from California to Wilkes-Barre!

Complicated Machinery

Once in the pencil factory—$4,000,000 in machinery and building, all capital accumulated by thrifty and saving parents of mine—each slat is given eight grooves by a complex machine, after which another machine lays leads in every other slat, applies glue, and places another slat atop—a lead sandwich, so to speak. Seven brothers and I are mechanically carved from this "wood-clinched" sandwich.

My "lead" itself—it contains no lead at all—is complex. The graphite is mined in Sri Lanka. Consider these miners and those who make their many tools and the makers of the paper sacks in which the graphite is shipped and those who make the string that ties the sacks and those who put them aboard ships and those who make the ships. Even the lighthouse keepers along the way assisted in my birth—and the harbor pilots.

The graphite is mixed with clay from Mississippi in which ammonium hydroxide is used in the refining process. Then wetting agents are added such as sulfonated tallow—animal fats chemically reacted with sulfuric acid. After passing through numerous machines, the mixture finally appears as endless extrusions—as from a sausage grinder—cut to size, dried, and baked for several hours at 1,850 degrees Fahrenheit. To increase their strength and smoothness the leads are then treated with a hot mixture which includes candelilla wax from Mexico, paraffin wax, and hydrogenated natural fats.

My cedar receives six coats of lacquer. Do you know all of the ingredients of lacquer? Who would think that the growers of castor beans and the refiners of castor oil are a part of it? They are. Why, even the processes by which the lacquer is made a beautiful yellow involve the skills of more persons than one can enumerate!

Observe the labeling. That's a film formed by applying heat to carbon black mixed with resins. How do you make resins and what, pray, is carbon black?

My bit of metal—the ferrule—is brass. Think of all the persons who mine zinc and copper and those who have the skills to make shiny sheet brass from these products of nature. Those black rings on my ferrule are black nickel. What is black nickel and how is it applied? The complete story of why the center of my ferrule has no black nickel on it would take pages to explain.

Then there's my crowning glory, inelegantly referred to in the trade as "the plug," the part man uses to erase the errors he makes with me. An ingredient called "factice" is what does the erasing. It is a rubber-like product made by reacting rape seed oil from the Dutch East Indies with sulfur chloride. Rubber, contrary to the common notion, is only for binding purposes. Then, too, there are numerous vulcanizing and accelerating agents. The pumice comes from Italy; and the pigment which gives "the plug" its color is cadmium sulfide.

No One Knows

Does anyone wish to challenge my earlier assertion that no single person on the face of this earth knows how to make me?

Actually, millions of human beings have had a hand in my creation, no one of whom even knows more than a very few of the others. Now, you may say that I go too far in relating the picker of a coffee berry in far off Brazil and food growers elsewhere to my creation, that this is an extreme position. I shall stand by my claim. There isn't a single person in all these millions, including the president of the pencil company, who contributes more than a tiny, infinitesimal bit of know-how. From the standpoint of know-how the only difference between the miner of graphite in Sri Lanka and the logger in Oregon is in the *type* of know-how. Neither the miner nor the logger can be dispensed with, any more than can the chemist at the factory or the worker in the oil field—paraffin being a by-product of petroleum.

Here is an astounding fact: Neither the worker in the oil field nor the chemist nor the digger of graphite or clay nor any who mans or makes the ships or trains or trucks nor the one who runs the machine that does the knurling on my bit of metal nor the president of the company performs his singular task because he wants me. Each one wants me less, perhaps, than does a child in the first grade. Indeed, there are some among this vast multitude who never saw a pencil nor would they know how to use one. Their motivation is other than me. Perhaps it is something like this: Each of these millions sees that he can thus exchange his tiny know-how for the goods and services he needs or wants. I may or may not be among these items.

No Master Mind

There is a fact still more astounding: the absence of a master mind, of anyone dictating or forcibly directing these countless actions which bring me into being. No trace of such a person can be found. Instead, we find the Invisible Hand at work. This is the mystery to which I earlier referred.

It has been said that "only God can make a tree." Why do we agree with this? Isn't it because we realize that we ourselves could not make one? Indeed, can we even describe a tree? We cannot, except in superficial terms. We can say, for instance, that a certain molecular configuration manifests itself as a tree. But what mind is there among men that could even record, let alone direct, the constant changes in molecules that transpire in the life span of a tree? Such a feat is utterly unthinkable!

I, Pencil, am a complex combination of miracles: a tree, zinc, copper, graphite, and so on. But to these miracles which manifest themselves in Nature an even more extraordinary miracle has been added: the configuration of creative human energies—millions of tiny know-hows configurating naturally and spontaneously in response to human necessity and desire and *in the absence of any human master-minding!* Since only God can make a tree, I insist that only God could make me. Man can no more direct these millions of know-hows to bring me into being than he can put molecules together to create a tree.

The above is what I meant when writing, "If you can become aware of the miraculousness which I symbolize, you can help save the freedom mankind is so unhappily losing." For, if one is aware that these know-hows will naturally, yes, automatically, arrange themselves into creative and productive patterns in response to human necessity and demand—that is, in the absence of governmental or any other coercive master-minding—then one will possess an absolutely essential ingredient for freedom: *a faith in free men*. Freedom is impossible without this faith.

Once government has had a monopoly of a creative activity such, for instance, as the delivery of the mails, most individuals will believe that the mails could not be efficiently delivered by men acting freely. And here is the reason: Each one acknowledges that he himself doesn't know how to do all the things incident to mail delivery. He also recognizes that no other individual could do it. These assumptions are correct. No individual possesses enough know-how to perform a nation's mail delivery any more than any individual possesses enough know-how to make a pencil. Now, in the absence of faith in free men—in the unawareness that millions of tiny know-hows would naturally and miraculously form and cooperate to satisfy this necessity—the individual cannot help but reach the erroneous conclusion that mail can be delivered only by governmental "master-minding."

Testimony Galore

If I, Pencil, were the only item that could offer testimony on what men can accomplish when free to try, then those with little faith would have a fair case. However, there is testimony galore; it's all about us and on every hand. Mail delivery is exceedingly simple when compared, for instance, to the making of an automobile or a calculator or a grain combine or a milling machine or to tens of thousands of other things.

The lesson I have to teach is this: Leave all creative energies uninhibited. Merely organize society to act in harmony with this lesson. Let society's legal apparatus remove all obstacles the best it can. Permit these creative know-hows freely to flow. Have faith that free men will respond to the Invisible Hand. This faith will be confirmed. I, Pencil, seemingly simple though I am, offer the miracle of my creation as testimony that this is a practical faith, as practical as the sun, the rain, a cedar tree, the good earth.

Letter To His Grandson
by Fred I. Kent
(for ages 12 and up)

Mr. Kent's grandson, then a schoolboy, was disturbed by the current fashion of disparaging the profit system. He had asked his grandfather to explain just how there can be a profit which is not taken from the work of someone else.

April 1942

My dear grandson:

I will answer your question as simply as I can. Profit is the result of enterprise which builds for others as well as for the enterpriser. Let us consider the operation of this fact in a primitive community, say of one hundred persons who are non-intelligent beyond the point of obtaining the mere necessities of living by working hard all day long.

Our primitive community, dwelling at the foot of a mountain, must have water. There is no water except at a spring near the top of the mountain: therefore, every day all the hundred persons climb to the top of the mountain. It takes them one hour to go up and back. They do this day in and day out, until at last one of them notices that the water from the spring runs down inside the mountain in the same direction that he goes when he comes down. He conceives the idea of digging a trough in the mountainside all the way down to the place where he has his habitation. He goes to work to build a trough. The other ninety-nine people are not even curious as to what he is doing.

Then one day this hundredth man turns a small part of the water from the spring into his trough and it runs down the mountain into a basin he has fashioned at the bottom. Whereupon he says to the ninety-nine others, who each spend an hour a day fetching their water, that if they will each give him the daily production of ten minutes of their time, he will give them water from his basin. He will then receive nine hundred and ninety minutes

of the time of the other men each day, which will make it unnecessary for him to work sixteen hours a day in order to provide for his necessities. He is making a tremendous profit—but his enterprise has given each of the ninety-nine other people fifty additional minutes each day for himself.

The enterpriser, now having sixteen hours a day at his disposal and being naturally curious, spends part of his time watching the water run down the mountain. He sees that it pushes along stones and pieces of wood. So he develops a water wheel; then he notices that it has power and, finally, after many hours of contemplation and work, makes the water wheel run a mill to grind his corn.

This hundredth man then realizes that he has sufficient power to grind corn for the other ninety-nine. He says to them, "I will allow you to grind your corn in my mill if you will give me one tenth the time you save." They agree, and so the enterpriser now makes an additional profit. He uses the time paid him by the ninety-nine others to build a better house for himself, to increase his conveniences of living through new benches, openings in his house for light, and better protection from the cold. So it goes on, as this hundredth man constantly finds ways to save the ninety-nine the total expenditure of their time—one tenth of which he asks of them in payment for his enterprising.

This hundredth man's time finally becomes all his own to use as he sees fit He does not have to work unless he chooses to. His food and shelter and clothing are provided by others. His mind, however, is ever working and the other ninety-nine are constantly having more time to themselves because of his thinking and planning.

For instance, he notices that one of the ninety-nine makes better shoes than the others. He arranges for this man to spend all his time making shoes, because he can feed him and clothe him and arrange for his shelter from profits. The other ninety-eight do not now have to make their own shoes. They are charged one tenth the time they save. The ninety-ninth man is also able to work shorter hours because some of the time that is paid by each of the ninety-eight is allowed to him by the hundredth man.

As the days pass, another individual is seen by the hundredth man to be making better clothes than any of the others, and it is arranged that his time shall be given entirely to his specialty. And so on.

Due to the foresight of the hundredth man, a division of labor is created that results in more and more of those in the community doing the things for which they are best fitted. Everyone has a greater amount of time at his disposal. Each becomes interested, except the dullest, in what others are doing and wonders how he can better his own position. The final result is that each person begins to find his proper place in an intelligent community.

But suppose that, when the hundredth man had completed his trough down the mountain and said to the other ninety-nine, "If you will give me what it takes you ten minutes to produce, I will let you get water from my basin," they had turned on him and said, "We are ninety-nine and you are only one. We will take what water we want. You cannot prevent us and we will give you nothing." What would have happened then? The incentive of the most curious mind to build upon his enterprising thoughts would have been taken away. He would have seen that he could gain nothing by solving problems if he still had to use every waking hour to provide his living. There could have been no advancement in the community. The same stupidity that first existed would have remained. Life would have continued to be a drudge to everyone, with opportunity to do no more than work all day long just for a bare living.

But we will say the ninety-nine did not prevent the hundredth man from going on with his think-

ing, and the community prospered. And we will suppose that there were soon one hundred families. As the children grew up, it was realized that they should be taught the ways of life. There was now sufficient production so that it was possible to take others away from the work of providing for themselves, pay them, and set them to teaching the young.

Similarly, as intelligence grew, the beauties of nature became apparent. Men tried to fix scenery and animals in drawings—and art was born. From the sounds heard in nature's studio and in the voices of the people, music was developed. And it became possible for those who were proficient in drawing and music to spend all their time at their art, giving of their creations to others in return for a portion of the community's production.

As these developments continued, each member of the community, while giving something from his own accomplishments, became more and more dependent upon the efforts of others. And, unless envy and jealousy and unfair laws intervened to restrict honest enterprisers who benefited all, progress promised to be constant.

Need we say more to prove that there can be profit from enterprise without taking anything from others, that such enterprise adds to the ease of living for everyone?

These principles are as active in a great nation such as the United States as in our imaginary community. Laws that kill incentive and cripple the honest enterpriser hold back progress. True profit is not something to be feared, because it works to the benefit of all.

We must endeavor to build, instead of tearing down what others have built. We must be fair to other men, or the world cannot be fair to us.

Sincerely,

Grandfather

The Cow in the Apartment
by Burton Rascoe*
(for ages 12 and up)

Helping yourself is one of the best possible ways to help others.

Haven't you at one time or another remarked, or heard, without protest, a friend remark: "Radio and TV would be all right if it weren't for the commercials," or "He used to be a pretty good writer, but he is turning out nothing but commercial stuff nowadays," or "Commerce and religion don't mix well," or "It's the commercial angle that is tied in with the project that I object to"?

If so, have you ever realized that every one of those expressions and others like them are nothing whatever but displays and airings of baseless and rather vulgar snobbery?

We are all—every single one of us—engaged in trade. Trade is our way of helping ourselves and others.

The man who deposits a bottle full of milk before my apartment door every morning is in trade, even though he belongs to a driver's union; and his being in trade is a way of helping me and others. Since I live in an apartment in the city, I can't keep a cow handy, even if I knew how to milk her. Even if it were possible for me to keep a cow in the apartment, the cow would produce more milk than I can use. I couldn't stop milking her; for if I did, she would go dry. I would have an unproductive cow on my hands in an apartment, and the cost of feeding and cleaning up after her would be great. If I tried to get back some of the cost by selling the surplus, I would have to go into business, buy bottles and sterilizing and pasteurizing chemicals and equipment, solicit customers, keep books, keep publicly displayed the O.P.A.** milk prices, file and pay quarterly income taxes, get, display

and keep paid up on, the necessary licenses, submit to regular federal, state, and municipal food and hygiene inspection, promptly report all symptoms of hoof-and-mouth disease, ticks or other cow afflictions, dun my delinquent customers, and Lord knows what all—and the surplus milk from one cow would cost me X-dollars for every 28¢ bottle of milk I sold.

So my milkman, in trade, helps me in more ways than he probably realizes; and he also helps so many other people. By helping the milk company to keep together, he even helps me to enjoy certain dramas on my TV. From the aggregate of profits in fractions of mills on the 28¢ bottle of milk, the company seeks to increase the number of persons it helps in the same way it does me.

One of the ways the company can increase its number of milk customers is by advertising; and one of these ways of advertising is by helping the television companies to keep in business by buying time from the companies for the televising of dramas for which writers, directors, producers, camera operators, electricians, costumers, make-up artists, script girls, announcers, and actors must be hired.

Every aspect of all this is commercial, from the creative talent of the writer of the drama, who trades the product of his brains for cash to the rest of the studio, to the work of the scrub woman who cleans up the studio. But the only thing that is labeled "commercial" is the selling-talk for the milk company, which appears at the beginning, in the middle, and at the end of the TV drama, and which consumes not more than three minutes of the TV audience's time.

Yet those three minutes are entirely devoted by the company to the helping of others — commercial script-writers, actors, scenic artists, cameramen, electricians, and others — all of whom are provided with a means of livelihood by the indispensable and economically justifiable "commercial" which makes it possible to see a good drama, well acted, without cost in my living room.

It is impossible honestly to make a great deal of money without doing a great deal of good.

* Burton Rascoe (1892-1957) was a literary critic/ free-lance writer.
**The O.P.A. (established 1941) now has its counterpart in the Price Commission, set up since the President's Wage-Price Freeze, announced August 15, 1971.

3. Start at the Beginning
by Robert LeFevre
(for ages 14 and up)

Were I called upon today to teach a course in basic economics, I would begin at the beginning. It is my observation that this procedure is rarely followed these days.

It has been my lot for a number of years to deal with management trainees for several companies, including one large corporation. Most of these trainees have come from some of our finest colleges and universities. Perhaps as many as twenty per cent have studied advanced economics, and a few hold degrees in the discipline. Probably as many as fifty per cent have received advanced degrees in one or another field. These young men and women are far above average. All are talented, a few gifted, and here and there an undoubted genius.

I work with eight hundred to a thousand people of this caliber every year. Perhaps one in a thousand can relate the myriad bits of data learned in school to the realities of human existence in this world.

Most arrive for my seminars with two economic assumptions of direful foreboding: (1) The large corporations represent a constant danger and must be controlled by the government; (2) Without antitrust laws, the Environmental Protection Agency and other bureaucratic interventions, private businessmen, large and small, would walk roughshod over the entire population of this country. The reason? Free enterprise leads inevitably to monopoly.

These seminar attendees did not invent these anxieties. They learned them at the feet of their professors, many of them professors in economics.

It is Futile to Argue

I have learned from experience that any attempt to dispute these conclusions by direct debate is largely futile. As the early rhymesters had it, "a man convinced against his will, is of the same opinion, still."

However, if I can go to the beginning to point out the realities undergirding all economic theory, then I have a chance of showing that an entirely different set of conclusions is warranted.

What then are these realities which should be seen at the beginning?

Or, even before that question is asked, what is the purpose of the study of economics?

Most of us are acquainted, perhaps by the process of a kind of social-intellectual osmosis, with the classical definition: economics is the study of the production, distribution and consumption of scarce resources. (**Note:** Currently the last two words are frequently replaced by the words "goods and services" and the concept of scarcity is omitted.)

While that definition is adequate, it lacks impact and immediacy. I would like to add to it a statement I must credit to Clark and Rimanoczy who pointed out nearly two score years ago that economics is the study of "How we live." That phrase brings it home and puts it on one's lap.

To understand economics is to understand how we take hold of the various resources of this world and put them together in such a way that we can stay alive. More. We do not, in economics, study merely the necessaries to retain the human heart beat. We want to survive, true. But we all want to live with some degree of personal satisfaction. To survive without any personal satisfactions would be to sustain a living death. Any prisoner in any jail receives the assurance that those who restrain him will do all in their power to keep him alive. That is not enough. We want to be alive as human beings, not as caged animals.

It follows that everyone, who wishes to stay alive as a human being, should understand at least the basics of economic lore. Those who have no such interest should wisely stop reading at this juncture.

Were I to teach economics, I would try to make these points clear.

What is the first reality we should recognize as soon as we have isolated our area of inquiry?

1. Man is a profit-seeking creature. I will not endeavor to prove that point at this time; rather, I state it categorically. However, I will embellish it enough to remove a common misunderstanding. The word profit is so affiliated with bookkeeping procedures that I can anticipate an assumption here. Some will be certain I have said that everyone wants to profit in terms of dollars. This is decidedly not so.

Many are not interested in dollars, as such. Whatever interest he might have in dollars, every human being seeks to obtain more of whatever it is he values. Conversely, he seeks to prevent the loss of anything he values.

I am using the term profit in a philosophic or even in a psychological sense. So I will introduce another term and use it in place of the word profit.

Every human being seeks **plus factors.** His plus factors may be dollars. But they might also be friendship, love, good health, a comfortable bed, a good meal, a rare book, a work of art, a day of leisure, a job, a good bridge game, or anything else his heart, body or mind desires. In this sense, man is a profit-seeker. He seeks to satisfy his desires whatever they may be.

2. Man lives in a world of limited (scarce) resources. Let me provide an illustration. Man is a land-using creature. His habitat is land, not air and not water. He uses air and water, but land is where he lives. Our planet has a limited supply of land. Approximately thirty per cent of the earth's surface is above water and not all of that readily habitable. The total population of the world, whatever it may be at any given moment, must use the resources of this world's land to survive and satisfy human needs and wants.

3. Not only is our world one of limited resources, the resources we do have are unevenly distributed. No two pieces of land are equal in terms of utilization. Some plots of land have multiple utility. Some are near water or receive rainfall. Some are not and do not. Some land contains minerals, oil, metals and various chemicals. Some is apparently barren in terms of our present knowledge and technology. In an attempt to be "fair," a division of the land so that each person would have an equal amount of acreage would be about as unfair as anything that could be imagined. The person receiving a few acres in the middle of the Gobi desert has a high probability of dying of thirst. The person receiving a few acres in the middle of Beverly Hills might do very well indeed.

4. The same diversity of distribution we find in land resources is found with human resources. Human beings are unevenly distributed about the globe. In a few places we will find millions of people living within a few square miles. Elsewhere we have zero population. Thus the distribution of human beings ranges from impacted, to dense, to settled, to sparse, to zip.

The same disequilibrium of human abilities is evident. Some persons can perform in a superior fashion at almost any endeavor or enterprise. Some have very meager competency. Most of us occupy the undistinguished center, capable or even superior at some tasks, bumblers or worse at others. And there are a few, always, who cannot manage.

Were I to attempt a teaching of economics, I would try to make the foregoing points clear. Much more could be said in every instance, of course.

There are a few more preliminaries.

5. All resources, capable of being owned, are property. Property is that item, real, personal or abstract, that can be identified as a thing in itself and is capable of being controlled by one or more humans under certain conditions. To survive and to survive with any hope of comfort and satisfaction it is necessary that each human being dominate his own environment in his own interest to some degree.

This is not only true of man, it is true of any living organism. Life, as we understand it, is only possible when a given entity is able to obtain what it needs from its surroundings. Nature has denied us the evidence of perpetual motion. Man is not born with a built-in power pack which makes him indifferent and independent of his surroundings. Even the sun is cooling.

6. Man is totally dependent upon property. He cannot survive without it. But property makes no decisions. All decisions over property are made by human beings who are capable of controlling that property under certain conditions. Nothing happens in the market automatically. If something is to be produced, someone must make a decision to produce it. If something is to be distributed, someone must make a decision to distribute it. If something is to be consumed, someone must make a decision to consume it.

In the absence of man, nature takes over and property obeys natural laws. When man is present, he learns natural law and, with that knowledge, exercises dominion over both natural and man-made properties.

7. Who is the proper decision maker over any given piece of property? A single choice is available. Either the person owning the property will make decisions over that property. Or a person not owning the property will make the decisions. Who else is there?

There are billions of pieces of property in the world. Each piece of property is owned by an individual or a group, or it is unowned. There are also billions of people in the world. If we decide that a nonowner should make the decisions over a property an individual owns, what incentive would there be for anyone to own anything? Further, which nonowner (when there are billions of nonowners in respect to each item owned) is to be given the authority over a property he doesn't own?

If we assume that all the nonowners should vote on each decision to be made, we reach the imponderability of numbers as well as the imponderability of information availability among those who are to vote. Indeed, we enter the theater of the absurd. Clearly, to reach decisions, either the owner or a selected group of nonowners must decide. The argument most often advanced in support of this latter practice is that private owners of property are profit-seekers and might make decisions that would injure others. Where is the evidence that nonowners are not profit-seekers? If I were called upon to make a decision over my neighbor's property, would I not be inclined to make a decision that would serve my ends, rather than my neighbor's?

While it is certainly true that the owner of a given item of property may lack in wisdom, it is equally true that a nonowner may also lack in wisdom.

But there is one thing to be said in favor of decision making by owners. To become an owner, certain thrift, forbearance and concern have already been expressed, either by the owner in person, or by those others who bestowed the property upon him and thus expect him to make decisions.

The only thing that can be said in favor of having nonowners make decisions over property they do not own is that they are there. But the owner is there, too.

8. Something needs to be said about decisions. Any decision is a finality. We cannot have it both ways. You cannot have your cake and eat it, too.

Are we to have homes only because others decide? Are we to wear clothing only when others make that decision? Are we to eat only when others reach that conclusion?

If you decide affirmatively in these last questions, then you have decided that man should be kept like an animal in a cage. And who decides which cage? Some other human being with no more wit nor wisdom than any other.

9. Finally, there is the question of right and wrong. I am not speaking of "good" or "bad." Good or bad are words derived from our respective value judgments. Right and wrong relate to appropriateness in terms of reality.

Without attempting a complete argument, because of space limitations, may I merely state categorically that there is only one way any human being can physically inflict an injury and hence impose a "wrong" on any other human being. He presumes to act as the authority over another person or that other person's property against that person's wishes. This is contrary to the basic nature of man as a profit-seeker. As a profit-seeker, each of us seeks to make decisions over his own person and property, and must do so to stay alive and

to achieve any measure of satisfaction. I am not speaking of children nor of any other incomplete or incompetent mentality. I speak of man qua man.

As a human being I am capable of either right or wrong behavior. That is to say, I can confine my decision-making to myself and my own resources in all categories. If I so limit my decision-making, it follows that I cannot commit a wrong against another. Since I do not presume to be an authority over anyone except myself, nor over any property except my own, my relationship with all others is peaceful and permits them to be free. Further, I am free, for the only person limiting my behavior is myself. And freedom means self-control.

When I am not content with this and presume to make decisions over other persons and other persons' property, and do so against their wills, then I am violating their basic natures as profit-seekers and am imposing wrongs upon them.

Were I to undertake the teaching of economics, I would begin with these beginnings. It is only when these ultimate givens are fully grasped and appreciated that we can enter the halls of the arcane mysteries provided by higher mathematics, calculus and statistical forecasting of probabilities. The economics professors may now take over. If they do so at this juncture, it is unlikely that they will presume the danger of the large corporation or the inevitability of monopoly, given a free market in a context of private ownership of property.

Reprinted with permission of the Foundation for Economic Education, 30 S. Broadway, Irvington-on-Hudson, New York 10533, web address: http://fee.org

Note: For further reading in regards to Number 7 in the above article *(Who is the proper decision maker over any given piece of property?)* read the following two articles: *Why Pay for Things?* (page 32) for ages 10 and up, and *Ownership Responsibility and the Child* (page 34) for ages 15 and up.

Why Pay For Things?

by F. A. Harper

(for parents, teachers, and others, ages 10 and up)

"Why do we have to pay for things?" asked a five-year-old boy at dinner one evening. Probably his question was prompted by the suffering of privation endured by all small boys, with their many wants to be served by few pennies. If unrestrained by either force or understanding, this condition can easily lead to theft.

This simple question caught father with his sheepskin up in the attic. So as a stall for time, the question was referred to an older sister who was a college student. Since she had never had a course in economics, it seemed safe to predict that she would fumble it for a few minutes.

She first asked how else it would be decided who should have things. And then she explained two choices—theft or payment for things—briefly but clearly. This approach struck me as an excellent alternative to either the rod or parental mandates by which children might be taught to respect the property of others. The argument, in amplified form, follows.

How might it be decided who gets what? There are not enough things to go around, you know. There never will be enough. We always want more things than there are to be had. Who will go without? Who will get what there is?

One way to do it would be for everyone to grab what he can. That is the way things tended to be done once, long before we were born. Under that way of doing things in its pure form, people fight over what little there is to be had. The man who works hard to get some food must either eat it at once or fight all the time to keep it. Nobody heeds his plea, that it is his because he worked to get it.

When things are done that way, you would not really own anything. You would just have it, and anyone could have it who could take it away from you. A boy's bicycle, for instance, would not really be his. Any bully could take it away from him; a bigger bully could take it away from the first thief, and so forth. People would lie and do all sorts of mean tricks to get things away from one another. The strongest and meanest and worst persons would get more and more things, so that most everyone would become meaner and meaner. Unless they did, they would have to go without things. They would have to be mean and physically strong, or die—under a system like that.

Who gets the bloody noses and broken heads under that system? Mostly it is the little folks of course, if they have anything anybody else wants and if they try to keep it. The old persons suffer, too, as do the crippled and the sick.

The other way to decide who gets what is for each person to own things. That is the system we have, generally. You own what you make. No bully has any right to it simply because he is big enough or mean enough to take it away from you. If he does take it, we say that it is still yours and he should return it to you.

Under this system, the person who makes anything may sell it or give it to other people. If as a small boy you had been given a bicycle, or had bought a toy ship, for instance, these are yours until you want to give them away or sell them. When they are sold, somebody must pay to get them.

That is why we have to pay for things. It is because we consider things to be owned by each person instead of belonging to nobody. If you want something you have not produced, and which has not been given to you, you must pay for it. The only other way to get it would be to steal it, which is the other system. People don't have to pay for things under the other system, but many starve because there are so few things produced.

It is normal for little boys, who want many things and don't have much money, to wonder why they should have to pay for things they want. But if we operated our affairs the other way and fought over things rather than owning them, little folks wouldn't have much of a chance of ever getting a bicycle at all.

The system whereby each person owns things—which means you have to pay for things you want—is really the cheapest and best police force in the world, in addition to being the only system that will defend the weak and the infirm. If we would all conduct ourselves by that rule, we would need no policemen at all because everybody would be serving as a policeman over himself. He then serves without pay. He can spend all his time producing things and enjoying life in whatever way seems best.

That answer to the question of why we have to pay for things, expressed in terms a five-year-old could understand, seemed to leave little more to be said.

Reprinted with permission of the Foundation for Economic Education, 30 S. Broadway, Irvington-on-Hudson, New York 10533, web address: http://fee.org

Ownership
Responsibility and the Child
by Gary North
(for parents, teachers, and others ages 15 and up)

Defenders of the free enterprise system may be rare, but there are a lot more of them than of those who practice freedom. There are always more entrepreneurs around than free enterprise advocates, but I am not talking about entrepreneurs. I am talking about the depressingly short supply of free enterprise defenders who make micro-economic decisions in terms of a philosophy of open competition on a price-oriented market. The temptation of temporary economic advantage lures capitalist after capitalist into the arms of the statist regulating agencies. The micro-economic decisions at the level of the individual and the firm are the crucial ones, and it is precisely here that the war against statism is being lost.

Yet, if the firm seems to be an area of retreat, the family is a philosophical disaster area. Men and women who are personally committed to the idea of the moral superiority of the voluntary market and private ownership seem incapable of grasping the parental role of imparting their faith to their children. The family is the training ground for children in every sphere of their young lives. Why should the concept of private ownership and personal responsibility be deferred until the child reaches his teens? If the first eight years are the crucial ones in the development of the child's perception of things, the establishment of his habits, the beginning of his intellectual tools, and the channeling of his emotions, then why are these years so ignored by parents as a time of training in the ideas of property?

Is there any concept that a child learns more rapidly than the concept of "mine?" I know virtually nothing of Soviet education at the preschool level, but I am certain that "correcting" this concept gives the teachers at the child day-care centers their most difficult intellectual problem. Unfortunately, the child does not seem to learn the equally important concept of "yours" with anything like the same facility. It would seem to be a moral problem with the child, not an intellectual one. That is why the authority of the parent is so vital in getting the child to acknowledge the validity of both of these interlocked concepts.

Children learn at astonishing rates of speed. All parents take pride in this fact, yet not one parent in a hundred really seems to understand just how fast his child does learn. The ability of a child to understand and act in terms of the most subtle human nuances—the look, the change of voice, a parent's weariness—is so great that it puts to shame whole teams of social psychologists and their computer cards...Children see and they remember differences between stated principles and demonstrated action. That is a child's means of survival, and he learns it very well and very early.

Parents for centuries have used the phrase, "Do as I say and not as I do," as a cover for their own moral weaknesses. A child may do just as his parent says, but in all likelihood he is thinking something very different. The mind of the child must be challenged by something more than brute force as he grows older; the sooner his mind is challenged, the better. Force, used to conquer a child's rebellious will, does not guarantee anything about the state of the child's thoughts. Yet, in the long run, the parent's real battle is for the mind of his child; and there are innumerable competing institutions that are in the business of intellectual conversion.....

The Responsibility of Ownership

If the concept of private property is worth defending, and if personal responsibility is the moral basis of private property, then the family must be the scene of the child's introduction to the responsibilities of ownership. Sadly, most parents have been so utterly compromised—morally compromised—by the collectivistic concept of "the well-integrated child" that they fail to take advantage of a marvelous opportunity to teach their children the meaning of responsible ownership. These same parents are later shocked to discover that their teenager has abandoned "bourgeois concepts of property and morality." The child drops out of his tax-supported university, joins a commune, and openly defies the parent to stop him. Of course he has no respect for such bourgeois concepts; he was never expected to adopt them! The family structure that produced him never rewarded him in terms of those concepts. He might have been expected to do well individually outside the family—in school, in athletics, and so forth—but not inside the family.

Take, for example, the idea of "sharing." All well-integrated children share their toys with their brothers and sisters and with all the other boys and girls they play with. "Let Billy play with your airplane, sweetheart." Now "sweetheart" may know very well that Billy is a semiprofessional demolitionist, but he is supposed to let Billy play with his airplane, whether or not it took him a week to build it. Or maybe "sweetheart" is just another Ebenezer Scrooge. It really does not matter one way or the other. If Mama enforces her request that Billy be allowed to play with the airplane, she has begun to undercut the idea of ownership in the mind of her child. A request is one thing; enforcement is another. The child should be given the right to ignore the request without physical reprisal from his mother or Billy.

The Child's Decision

The parent can always give a whole barrage of cogent reasons why sharing is preferable to stinginess: people do not like selfish people, people will not share their toys with selfish people (which is, I think, the really effective argument), selfish people are mean, selfish people become social outcasts. Yet, the child is simultaneously informed that it is impossible to buy people's friendship. It is up to him to balance these competing propositions in his own mind...In any case, the decision ought to be the child's. If there are social costs associated with being selfish, let the child find out for himself, and let him evaluate them in terms of his own psychic needs. Maybe he likes toys better than friends... But it will have been his option, and he will have borne the costs. That is what the free society is all about. It cannot guarantee that everyone will grow up liked...but it can see to it that everyone pays his own share.

Group Relationships

Children are not stupid concerning group relationships. They understand why and how their peers operate. They have a larger stake in this kind of understanding than their parents could have...A child's concentration is focused. He learns to predict how his actions will be received. He may not act in terms of what he knows, but he is continually learning. If he thinks that he ought to share with others, he will. He can test his parents' remarks about the benefits of sharing. If he likes the results, fine; if not, he bears the costs. It is a very good, and from the parent's point of view, very inexpensive form of training.

If the parent continually interferes with the right of the child to do what he wants with his own property, he is setting up the child for every kind of collectivist panacea. He will learn that titles to property are less valid than the ability to manipulate the authorities to your own purposes. He will learn that the authorities cannot be trusted to fulfill their promises with respect to ownership. He will learn that "yours" really is not that fundamental a concept, since "mine" is not enforced either...

In Matters of Property

If a child is not taught the meaning of personal responsibility from the beginning, the family has failed in part of its function. That is why enforced sharing is so insidious. It destroys the links between ownership, power, and responsibility. The parent who makes his child share anything with anyone for any reason...is courting long-run rebellion. He can suggest; he dare not enforce.

...I have seen parents spend whole evenings trying to straighten out what can only be described as property disputes among children. Hours and hours of listening to "Johnny took my fire engine," and "Bobby took my Baby Jane Throw-up Doll," and "Well, she won't give me back my Frankenstein monster." It must drive them crazy, as it does me; but I can go home later on... if the parent sets himself up as the allocator of children's scarce resources, he can expect to spend a lot of time at that task.

Watch the Vigilante

There is one justification that is used by children for every kind of deviation: "He wouldn't give my toy to me, so I ...." A parent who stands ready to enforce the right of property in his household will not have to listen to that one; he can punish both the thief (for that is what he is) and the vigilante who retaliated. He can encourage victims to come to him because they can trust him to uphold them in their arguments. We expect that much as adults from the civil authorities; we should provide it in that sphere where we are the officials. We should

be able to be trusted, day in and day out, to render justice, whether we are tired, happy, sour, busy. The regularity of justice, the very predictability of it, is...respected by the child...It takes self-discipline in an adult to provide this kind of regularity; that is why there is truth to the phrase that delinquent parents are the chief cause of delinquent children. The lack of self-discipline becomes a heritage of families throughout several generations.

Applying the Principles

The defense of the free market cannot be made simply in terms of charts and graphs and technical explanations of market efficiency by professional economists. It must be defended by a willingness on the part of its supporters to understand its principles and apply them in all the relevant spheres of their personal lives...Indeed; if a parent is not willing to take the time to apply the principles that he professes to hold most dear within the confines of the institution that he holds most dear, he is not serious about his commitment to those principles. If parents use the family as a zone of safety from the responsibility of laboring to apply basic moral principles, then they should be ready to see their children on television during the mass arrests at the local university. If the principles of private ownership and personal responsibility are not worth teaching by word and example to one's children, they are not worth teaching at all.

Condensed and reprinted with permission of the Foundation for Economic Education, 30 S. Broadway, Irvington-on-Hudson, New York 10533, web address: http://fee.org

Note: For further reading in regards to the section titled *In Matters of Property* in the article above, read the article: *Free Market: Elementary, My Child* (page 37) for ages 12 and up.

Free Market: Elementary, My Child

by Barbara H. Bryan
(for parents, teachers, and others ages 12 and up)

Interventionist?

Who me—Free Market Mama?

Confession being good for the soul, I'll have to admit that I almost slipped—consciously at that—into an interventionist role.

And, candidly, had the reverse order of the following story occurred, I would have.

It happened when a 25-cent toy stamper (it inked pairs of black feet on any surface it touched) went through a price rise of some 1100 per cent within a few hours in our home.

The stamper was given to Jim Dixon by his grandmother. His buddies were enchanted when he decorated them with little black feet.

Their mothers may have been somewhat less delighted, but Jim Dixon was a trendsetter with fellow first graders. Therefore, the item had even more appeal.

Jim is a special friend and favorite of my three sons. They are with him in Sunday School and around the neighborhood. Last year he and Callan were in kindergarten together. Russ (Callan's twin) was in first grade with him this year. Big Brother Eason, a second grader, also thinks Jim is cool. The stamper represented the last word to all of them.

So when Russ came home and announced that he had just purchased the stamper for one dollar, I noted that he had made a willing exchange in a "seller's market." He could not have been happier. Jim realized he had struck a good bargain, so we all grinned.

About an hour later, Callan emptied his piggy bank and told me that he had to have enough money for 28 pieces of bubble gum. He said he only had enough "cents" for 23 pieces.

Assuming that he wanted everyone (20 classmates, hmmm?) in his class to have a piece, I offered him a window-washing job for a dime. Using the best of Tom Sawyer technique, he engaged Nicky and Wilson forthwith and managed it with great dispatch.

Soon he left with his full complement of cash. The story extends slightly because the convenience store clerk quite accidentally shortchanged him. With his finest eyes-just-above-the-counter aplomb he returned to the store and evened the score. Soon the bubble gum had been turned over to its new owner.

That person, it turned out, was his twin brother Russ, who for the bubble gum and two one-dollar bills released title to the stamper.

The story might have ended there. Nobody was interested in my suggestion that we telephone Jim's grandmother to ask where she had bought the feet stamper. Big Brother, usually shrewd and definitely well-heeled, entered the picture.

Simply because of his status as first-born, he had amassed a much fatter passbook savings account than his siblings. And, frankly, he gets a little horsey about his couple of hundred extra dollars.

#1[1]   Anyway, supply and demand being what they were that day, he and Callan wound up in a fascinating trading session. When we sat down to dinner, they had already agreed that Eason would fork over three dollars for the one-of-its-kind (at least in our house at that minute) item.

Knowing beyond question that he held all the cards, Callan savored his rare upper hand by playing wishy-washy. He said he might change his mind. He thought about upping the ante. He even said he might trade back with Russ and get his money returned.

We noted with three dollars he could repay himself and buy *more than* 28 pieces of gum. Eason was becoming nervous.

(At that point they counted the bubble gum and Russ The Casual learned that he had been shorted by three pieces which Callan admitted to sharing with his fellow window washers.)

My only intervention was to compliment them on their practice of free market economy. We did discuss supply and demand—*and* rampant inflation. And, I did suggest that a bargain struck should be honored. Translated: Callan shouldn't weasel out if Eason really wanted to pay that exorbitant figure—with his educated eyes open.

---

[1] The #1 appears here as an example for the suggested exercise that appears on page 11.

Had the reverse occurred—Eason preying upon Callan who would have hoodwinked Russ who would foist the stamper off on Jim—I would have envisioned all kinds of repercussions. And I probably would have intervened to save *my* face and to keep peace with the Dixons.

As far as I can tell, all four boys in the story are still smiling.

Jim's banker father must be proud of him. Russ and Callan have worked out a rental agreement with Eason so that they still have access to the black feet—for 10 cents an hour. Eason guards the thing with his life.

And Mom?

Well, so far I've found black feet stamped all over my car's Virginia license plate, the top of our living room fan, our back door neighbor's usually spotless child's face ("He *said* he wanted it there!") and the front of the bathroom door.

Perhaps I may end up paying for permitting that demonstration of "free" enterprise.

If we can get the point across with elbow grease, scrub on!

Reprinted with permission of the Foundation for Economic Education, 30 S. Broadway, Irvington-on-Hudson, New York 10533, web address: http://fee.org

For Discussion

Explain the difference between needs and wants. Have students list examples by making two columns. Mark one column "Needs" and the other column "Wants." Itemize "needs" and "wants" under the appropriate categories.   Example: Children need nutritious food. They do not need ice cream, candy, or soda, which usually fall under the category of wants. Why is it important to understand the difference?

Needs	**Wants**
nutritious food	ice cream

You should now begin to read
WHATEVER HAPPENED TO PENNY CANDY?

Be sure to read the "Preface" and "A Note About Economics".

Also, read the exercise on page 87, *A Personalized Consumer Price Index*.
If you decide to do this project, begin your research at this time.

NOTE: When defining vocabulary, the student is encouraged to use definitions found in the chapters and/or in the glossary of WHATEVER HAPPENED TO PENNY CANDY.

Preface

Short Answer/Fill-in/True or False

1. On what school (or schools) of economic theory is the book WHATEVER HAPPENED TO PENNY CANDY based?

2. What are the origins of the terms for these schools of economic theory?

3. Name individuals who are representative of these schools of economic theory. List the name of the individual, then next to that name list the school of economic theory each individual represents.

Discussion/Essay/Assignment

4. Call several of the local high schools in your area. Ask the economics teachers on what school of economics their high school text is based. If they need further clarification, provide a multiple choice answer: Keynesian, Monetarist, Austrian. (Note: Most school textbooks are based on Keynesian economics.) You can make the same inquiry of your local community colleges, 4-year colleges, or universities. Record and discuss your findings.

A Note About Economics

Short Answer/Fill-in/True or False

1. According to Uncle Eric, this book is based on _____ and _____ economics because good science and good economics depends upon the ability to _____.

Chapter 1: Money: Coins and Paper

Define

1.   Clad:

2.   Fine silver:

3.   Base metal:

4.   Token:

Short Answer/Fill-in/True or False

5.   Are coins dated 1965 to the present really coins? Explain.

Discussion/Essay/Assignment

6.   Refer to the Economic Timetable that appears on the final pages of the BLUESTOCKING GUIDE: ECONOMICS. In what year was silver removed from U.S. dimes and quarters? In what year was all gold backing removed from the U.S. dollar?

For Research

7.   For a week, each evening, sort all the coinage collected by each member of the family. Return all the coins dated after 1965. Ask to be able to borrow any coins dated before 1965. Assure their owner they will be returned at the end of a week, and then be sure to return them on the agreed upon date. At the end of the week, record how many pre-1965 coins you've found. Discuss your findings.

Chapter 2: Tanstaafl, the Romans, and Us

Define

1.   Double-digit inflation:

2.   Welfare program:

3.   Subsidy:

4.   Law of economics:

5.   Tanstaafl:

6.   Counterfeiting:

7.   Clipping:

8.   Reeding:

9.   Debasing:

10. Gresham's Law:

Short Answer/Fill-in/True or False

11. During a double-digit inflation explain what happens to the cost of a paperback book next year that costs $5.00 this year.

12. Why do governments tax its citizens?

13. Refer to the Economic Timetable. In what year did the Federal government assume the national debt following the American Revolution? How did the Federal government intend to raise the revenue to pay off the debt?

14. Refer to the Economic Timetable. What was each person's share of the national debt in 1791?   (Use the 1790 U.S. population figure for this exercise.)

15. How does a government counterfeit?

16. Refer to the Economic Timetable. What paper currency became worthless in 1781?

17.   Prior to printing presses, how did the Roman government counterfeit?

18.   Prior to 1965 which coins were reeded and which were not? Why?

19.   Today's dimes, quarters, and half dollars are reeded. Why are they reeded if they contain no silver?

20.   As in Ancient Rome, coins in the U.S. have been debased. In 1964 a half-dollar was 90% silver. Five years later it was down to 40%. Today it contains no silver. If America's coinage today has no intrinsic value, why does the American consumer take it in trade for goods and services?

21.   What would you do if a silver coin came into your possession today? Would you spend it, or save it? If lots of people save precious metal coins and spend the coins that are worth little, what law are they following? What does the law mean?

22.   Refer to the Economic Timetable. What event occurred in 1878 that set Gresham's Law into motion?

23.   Referring back to Question #7, Chapter #1, can you explain why you could find no precious metal coins in a week's accumulation of change?

Discussion/Essay/Assignment

24.   What might happen to a taxpayer who refuses to pay taxes because the tax money will go to support a government program with which the taxpayer disagrees?

25.   Why do you think people save precious metal coins? If precious metal coins are saved and not spent, what good can they be to people?

For Research (Discuss findings or write an essay)**:**

26.   Record the instances in which you hear someone say, "It's free! It doesn't cost anything." Who says it's free? (i.e., news commentator, commercial spokesperson, friend, neighbor, etc.) What product or service is free? Is it really free? If not, who really pays for it?

27.   Read the article on page 44, *How Government Intervention Plagued Our 19th-Century Economy*. Then research more about the 1878 Bland-Allison Act. You might compare the history of this event as it is explained by a free market writer (i.e. Lawrence W. Reed) versus a writer with an opposing viewpoint, or as explained in a modern encyclopedia. What are the differences, if any, in the explanations of this event?

To View

The following movies make statements regarding taxation and subsidies:

28. *Harry's War.* 1981 comedy starring Edward Hermann, Geraldine Page, Karen Grassle, and David Ogden Stiers. Directed by Kieth Merrill. Harry Johnson, a mild-mannered postman, declares war on the Internal Revenue Service because they unfairly bill his "Aunt" Beverly over $192,000 in back taxes. Emphasis is on the lack of rights taxpayers have when confronted by the excessive abuse of power that is exercised by the IRS. All Harry wants is a trial by his peers as guaranteed by the U.S. Constitution. Rated PG. **For discussion:** Explain where you agree or disagree with Harry Johnson and his efforts to get the IRS to reconsider his "Aunt" Beverly's back tax bill.

29. *You Can't Take It With You.* 1938 comedy starring James Stewart, Jean Arthur, and Lionel Barrymore. Directed by Frank Capra. RCA/Columbia Pictures Home Video. Academy Award for Best Picture and Directing, 1938. Excellent scene in which Grandpa is confronted by an IRS man for not paying taxes for 20 odd years. Grandpa delivers a gratifying, and economically-satisfying response. **For discussion:** Do you agree with Grandpa's reasons for not paying taxes? If he receives nothing of value in return for payment of taxes, should he have to pay taxes? Should he be forced to pay taxes? Should he have to go to jail if he doesn't pay taxes? Does Grandpa refuse to pay all taxes, or does he agree to pay taxes, so long as he gets something he values in return, which he perceives as a fair exchange?

30. *Mr. Deeds Goes to Town.* 1936 comedy starring Gary Cooper. Directed by Frank Capra. **For discussion:** What is significant about the scene in which subsidizing the arts is discussed? Should every organization be self-supporting in order to justify its own existence? For example, if an organization, whose sole purpose is to enlighten, educate or inform, cannot survive without the contributions of government or private benefactors, should it exist? Explain your answer. What is the difference, if any, between voluntary contributions versus forced contributions? Explain.

For Further Reading

31. *How Government Intervention Plagued Our 19th-Century Economy* (next page) by Lawrence W. Reed (for ages 16 and up).

32. *A King of Long Ago* by Lewis Love (for ages 12 and up) in ECONOMICS: A FREE MARKET READER, published by Bluestocking Press, phone: 800-959-8586, web site: www.BluestockingPress.com

33. *Not Yours to Give* by David Crockett (for ages 14 and up) in ECONOMICS: A FREE MARKET READER, published by Bluestocking Press, phone: 800-959-8586, web site: www.BluestockingPress.com

How Government Intervention
Plagued Our 19th-Century Economy
by Lawrence W. Reed
(for ages 16 and up)

The recessions and depressions of the 19th century are often cited as proof of the "inherent instability" of the free market. (Indeed, the promoters of the Federal Reserve System in 1913 argued for a central bank as a way of preventing future downturns!) This is, of course, a bum rap.

The 1800s were freer than today, but there was more than enough government intervention to cause serious setbacks in the economy. And Austrian trade cycle theory explains exactly how.

The source of the business cycle, Mises discovered, is government-engineered expansion of money and credit. Such a policy artificially depresses interest rates at first, deranges the structure of production by generating unsustainable malinvestments, and inevitably leads to contraction and painful readjustments.

The first economic calamity of the century occurred in 1808 when a federal embargo on overseas shipping produced widespread bankruptcies and unemployment. After that, four major cyclical depressions struck the American economy: in 1819, 1837, 1857, and 1893. The typical economic history text lists among the "causes" things like railroad speculation, stock crashes, trade imbalances, commodity price booms and busts, etc.

These are not, of course, causes at all, but merely symptoms. Only Austrian trade cycle theory as propounded by Ludwig von Mises, Murray N. Rothbard, and others, makes sense of the mess and provides a coherent explanation of these five depressions.

The 1819 collapse followed a flagrant credit expansion by the Second Bank of the United States, created by the feds in 1816. The definitive work on the experience is still Rothbard's Ph.D. thesis, *The Panic of 1819.*

Rothbard documented the extensive culpability of the Second Bank. In its very first year, it issued $23 million on a specie reserve of about $2.5 million. The expansion of credit, which eventually involved state banks as well, was actively encouraged by the U.S. Treasury. The government even made it legal for inflating banks to fraudulently suspend payment of specie, ripping off hapless depositors in the process.

Then, in a series of deliberate deflationary moves, the Second Bank pulled the rug out from under the very house of cards it had built. It forced a drastic reduction in the money supply starting as early as the middle of 1818. The depression, which came a few months later, was the unavoidable outcome of gross manipulation of money and credit.

Those who blame the gold standard for this debacle are wrong. In fact, the country was not even on a gold standard at the time. In 1792, the official policy was "bimetallism," according to which silver and gold were to circulate side by side at a governmentally fixed ratio. (The ratio between the prices of any two commodities, including gold and silver, is always changing on the market, and an attempt to fix the ratio by government fiat always leads to trouble. In this instance, it forced the country onto a de facto silver standard from the start. The same sort of intervention proved to be a major factor in the later crisis of 1893.)

The Second Bank's shenanigans created the depression of 1837. Anticipating a political battle to renew the Bank when its charter ran out in 1836, Bank authorities early in the decade embarked upon a rapid expansion of the money supply. Reserve ratios were pushed to their lowest levels of the entire antebellum period. Orchestrating "good times" through easy money was the Bank's way of fighting hard-money, anti-central bank President Andrew Jackson.

Jackson, however, flattened the inflation by requiring specie in payment for federal lands and by vetoing the Bank's charter. In the quick contraction that followed, the inflationary malinvestments promoted by the bank were liquidated. But Washington persisted with its policy of bimetallism. In addition, state and local governments responded to the 1837 collapse with a wave of anti-banking laws, outlawing banks altogether in some places and exacerbating the depression. This is hardly laissez-faire or gold standard behavior.

By the early 1850s, state governments got into the inflation act. Exerting control over their extensive network of state-chartered banks, they pressured the banks to monetize state debt. The result was another round of credit expansion, dangerous reduction of specie reserves, and a temporary, artificial boom in the economy, followed by panic and depression in 1857. Because the pressure on banks to monetize debt occurred principally in the Northern states, the subsequent collapse was considerably less pronounced in the South.

The general depression of 1873 also provides a clear example of government as the guilty party. In the prior decade, both Northern and Southern regimes abandoned a specie standard altogether and printed massive quantities of irredeemable, legal tender paper.

In the Confederacy, high taxes, a paper hyperinflation, and Northern scorched-earth military policies plunged the region into depression in 1865.

In the North, despite crippling tax hikes, revenues fell far short of the funds necessary to prosecute the war. No less than $5.2 billion in "greenbacks" were printed. At the war's conclusion, a greenback dollar was worth only 35 cents in gold. The Northern economy struggled for a few more years, but with the complete cessation of paper inflation in the 1870s, collapse and readjustment began by 1873.

Recovery had barely commenced when the central government began a new form of monetary intervention, this one tied to silver. In 1878, Congress passed (over President Hayes' veto) the Bland-Allison Act, which mandated the Treasury's purchase of $2-4 million in silver bullion per month. The metal was to be minted into silver dollars, each containing 371.25 grains of silver. Since the gold dollar was defined as 23.22 grains of gold, this established a ratio between the two metals of 16 to 1.

But the free market value of silver in terms of gold was at least 18 to 1 in 1878. By overvaluing silver and undervaluing gold, Bland-Allison set Gresham's Law into motion. "Bad" money (officially overvalued silver) began to drive "good" money (officially undervalued gold) out of circulation, deranging the nation's finances and engendering a steady loss of confidence in the currency. On top of it all, Bland-Allison authorized the Treasury to issue paper silver certificates along with the depreciating silver dollars.

The inflationists of the period—who pushed for this intervention in the belief that "more money" would aid the economy in general and debtors in particular—were not satisfied. Throughout the 1880s, they pushed for even more inflation under the guise of "doing something for silver."

Their crowning folly was enacted into law in 1890—the Sherman Silver Purchase Act. It required the Treasury to buy virtually the entire output of American silver mines—4.5 million ounces per month; mint it at 16 to 1 at a time when the gold/silver ratio in the free market was actually greater than 30 to 1; and issue new paper "Treasury Notes" simultaneously.

Drugged by easy money, the economy took on the classic symptoms of a boom. Unemployment and interest rates in 1891 and 1892 fell dramatically. Capital goods industries worked feverishly. Foreigners, however, were the first to sense danger and began withdrawing their capital from America as early as 1891.

The economic reversal started in 1893, and led to the worst depression in 50 years. It also produced one of the more scholarly addresses ever delivered before the House of Representatives. Congressman Bourke Cochran of New York, a first-rate historian, traced the history of coinage in England and explained how debasing the currency led to recurrent depressions. Applying that principle to his day, he declared:

> I think it safe to assert that every commercial crisis can be traced to an unnecessary inflation of the currency, or to an improvident expansion of credit. The operation of the Sherman Law has been to flood this country with paper money without providing any method whatever for its redemption. The circulating medium has become so redundant that the channels of commerce have overflowed and gold has been expelled.

Viewing the crisis of 1893, contemporary historian Ernest Ludlow Bogart said:

It must be said that the net results of this experiment of "managed currency," that is, one in which the government undertakes to provide the necessary money for the people, were disastrous. For the maintenance of a suitable supply, the operation of normal economic forces is more reliable than the judgment of a legislative body.

The economy of 19th-century America was punctuated by serious economic setbacks. They were caused not by the free market, but by the destructive manipulations and interventions of government authorities. This was not a century of government as innocent bystander, but of government as the incessant bungler, running roughshod over the principle of sound and honest money. (Although, without a Fed and other government interventions, the recoveries from these panics were quick.)

We can learn much from the experiences sketched here. Monetary reform, if it is to be genuine and successful, must sever money and banking from politics. That's why a modern gold standard must have: no central bank; no fixed ratios between gold and silver; no bail-outs; no suspension of gold payments or other bank frauds; no monetization of debt; and no inflation of the money supply, all of which have proved so disastrous in the past.

Anything short of the discipline and honesty of a true gold coin standard will inevitably self-destruct, consuming our wealth and liberties, and nurturing the omnipotent state.

Reprinted from *The Free Market*, November 1987 issue, with permission of the Ludwig von Mises Institute, 518 West Magnolia Avenue, Auburn, AL 36832-4528, web address: mises.org

Chapter 3: Inflation

Define

1.   Law of supply and demand:

2.   Inflation:

Short Answer/Fill-in/True or False

3.   Which statement is true?
       A. Inflation causes rising prices.
       B. Inflation is rising prices.

4.   List examples of the law of supply and demand that you can identify from your own experiences.

For Research (Discuss findings or write an essay)**:**

5.   Research the value of various currencies, foreign and American, over the past 30 years. Conduct an internet search for the data. (As I write this today a current site is: Lawrence H. Officer, "Exchange Rates Between the United States Dollar and Forty-one Currencies,", MeasuringWorth, 2009. URL: http://www.measuringworth.org/exchangeglobal.) On a separate piece of paper, chart the rise and fall in the values at six-month intervals. As the value of the currencies fall, what happens to the price of goods that you might be successful in tracking? If the value of the currencies rise, what happens to the values of goods?

6.   Secure a copy of an old mail order catalog. Dover Publications publishes a Montgomery Ward 1895 catalog (ISBN 0-486-223779). Make two columns on a sheet of paper. The heading for column one will be the year of your primary source publication, i.e., 1895 in the case of the Montgomery Ward catalog. Column two will be the current year. Along the left-hand side of the paper, make a list of the products whose prices you are comparing. Compare the price of the products advertised in 1895 to their price today. What do you think accounts for the price differences?

7.   Ask your parents what the price of certain items were when they were young. For example, when Richard Maybury (Uncle Eric) was a boy, a typical factory worker's starting wage in his home town was $0.50 per hour, and the highest wage for a factory worker at that time was $0.96 per hour. Candy cost a penny. Movies cost a dime. Bread cost $0.15. By contrast, when Uncle Eric's father was a boy, bread cost $0.05. What does an average loaf of bread cost today? How much does it cost to see a movie at the theater?

8.   Refer to the Economic Timetable. Starting in 1926 record the price of five pounds of flour in 1926, 1945, and 1988. What is the price of five pounds of flour today?

9.   Refer to the Economic Timetable. What was the supply of money in circulation in 1920 and in 1945? What is it today? A suggested web site for this research is: http://www.federalreserve.gov/releases/h6/current/

For Further Reading

10.   *Inflation is...* by Beth A. Hoffman (for ages 10 and up), see below.

11.   *Inflation in One Page* by Henry Hazlitt (for ages 16 and up), see page 50 of this book.

12.   *How Much Money?* by Percy L. Greaves, Jr. (for ages 15 and up) in ECONOMICS: A FREE MARKET READER, published by Bluestocking Press, phone: 800-959-8586, web site: www.BluestockingPress.com

Inflation is . . .
by Beth A. Hoffman
(for ages 10 and up)

Dear M_____:

Thank you for your letter, asking for information about inflation. The members of the staff here at The Foundation for Economic Education have been studying inflation for many years. We have published books and many articles about the subject. I will share with you some of the things I have learned.

Government causes inflation by printing lots of paper dollars. Many people believe that inflation is high prices. But actually inflation is the increase in the quantity of money. How does this increase lead to high prices?

Well, let's pretend that you're not happy with the allowance that your parents give you. You don't have enough money to buy all the bubble gum, hamburgers, comics or toys that you want. Let's also suppose that you had a...Machine that could print all the dollars you wanted. (This is called "counterfeiting" and people go to jail for doing this. But just pretend that you could print as much money as you'd like.) Since you would have all the dollars from this...Machine you could spend as much as you like and would not have to worry about asking your family for a bigger allowance. When you're on a limited allowance you have to watch your pennies pretty carefully. But if you had a...Machine, you could be less careful with your dollars. You wouldn't have to choose between a new book and a pad of drawing paper. You could buy *both* — and even more! This would be fine and dandy for a time.

But suppose your friends all had these...Machines—or that you had so many dollars that you gave a lot of them to your friends. Well, if enough of you had loads of money to spend at the local candy store pretty soon something interesting would happen. The candy store owner has only a certain amount of bubble gum to sell. But suddenly, with you and other "rich" kids, there's a *big* demand for bubble gum! If he had only 5 packages of gum for sale and there were ten of you who wanted to buy it, any one of you might be willing to pay $10.00 or more for one package of gum. (Remember that back when you had only your allowance, you'd *never* pay that much for a little pack of gum!) Because of the bigger demand, the owner of the candy store might decide to ask a higher price for the gum—and you will pay it because each of your dollars has lost some of its value. You may seem "rich" but your money has lost a lot of its buying power because there are others who also have lots of money and are "rich."

In very simple terms, this is what our government has done. Through many decisions made by the officials in the government, there has been an increase in the number of dollars printed. There are just many more dollars—paper dollars that don't buy as much as the old dollars did. (You've probably heard adults say "Gee, the dollar doesn't go as far as it used to.")

The people in this country give the government its "allowance" by paying taxes. But taxes are not popular. So, rather than asking for a bigger "allowance," that is, for higher taxes, the government tries something else. It prints money with a printing machine. And when the government does it, it's legal! Because it can legally print almost as many dollars as it wants, the government doesn't have to go to the people and say, "We need more money to pay soldiers and policemen and to buy all the things we want to give people." The officials can print more money to pay all their debts. And they can print more money to pay for lots of benefits for their friends. And if they can't print enough, they can ask for an "advance" on next year's "allowance." This way, people don't have to pay more taxes, the government can hand out goodies and everyone seems happy. But eventually everyone begins to realize that the dollars are not worth what they once were. And, just as with your...Money Machine, the government's money machine doesn't make everyone rich. Some people seem rich for a while. But when some of the people get some of the newly printed dollars, they bid prices up. Then many other people can't buy the things they want. And so on.

I'm enclosing some articles you might want to read, particularly one by Mr. Henry Hazlitt, "Inflation in One Page." In different language, he says the same thing I've told you. When you are a bit older, you may also want to read Mr. Hazlitt's book called *Economics in One Lesson*.

If you have any questions or would like some more information, please write to me. I will try my best to help.

Cordially,
Beth Hoffman

Condensed and reprinted with permission of the Foundation for Economic Education, 30 S. Broadway, Irvington-on-Hudson, New York 10533, web address: http://fee.org

Inflation in One Page
by Henry Hazlitt
(for ages 16 and up)

A correspondent, heading a group of "Inflation Fighters," recently sent me a one-page typewritten summary of their case against inflation, and asked for my opinion of it. The statement was sincere and well-intentioned, but as with the great bulk of what is being written about inflation, it was confused in both its analysis and its recommendations.

I wrote approving his effort to "do something," and approving also his idea of trying to state the cause and cure for inflation on a single page, but suggested the following substitute statement:

Cause and Cure of Inflation

1. Inflation is an increase in the quantity of money and credit. Its chief consequence is soaring prices. Therefore inflation—if we misuse the term to mean the rising prices themselves—is caused solely by printing more money. For this the government's monetary policies are entirely responsible.

2. The most frequent reason for printing more money is the existence of an unbalanced budget. Unbalanced budgets are caused by extravagant expenditures which the government is unwilling or unable to pay for by raising corresponding tax revenues. The excessive expenditures are mainly the result of government efforts to redistribute wealth and income—in short, to force the productive to support the unproductive. This erodes the working incentives of both the productive and the unproductive.

3. The causes of inflation are not, as so often said, "multiple and complex," but simply the result of printing too much money. There is no such thing as "cost-push" inflation. If, without

an increase in the stock of money, wage or other costs are forced up, and producers try to pass these costs along by raising their selling prices, most of them will merely sell fewer goods. The result will be reduced output and loss of jobs. Higher costs can only be passed along in higher selling prices when consumers have more money to pay the higher prices.

4. Price controls cannot stop or slow down inflation. They always do harm. Price controls simply squeeze or wipe out profit margins, disrupt production, and lead to bottlenecks and shortages. All government price and wage control, or even "monitoring," is merely an attempt by the politicians to shift the blame for inflation on to producers and sellers instead of their own monetary policies.

5. Prolonged inflation never "stimulates" the economy. On the contrary, it unbalances, disrupts, and misdirects production and employment. Unemployment is mainly caused by excessive wage rates in some industries, brought about either by extortionate union demands, by minimum wage laws (which keep teenagers and the unskilled out of jobs), or by prolonged and over-generous unemployment insurance.

6. To avoid irreparable damage, the budget must be balanced at the earliest possible moment, and not in some sweet by-and-by. Balance must be brought about by slashing reckless spending, and not by increasing a tax burden that is already undermining incentives and production.

Reprinted with permission of the Foundation for Economic Education, 30 S. Broadway, Irvington-on-Hudson, New York 10533, web address: http://fee.org

Real Investment Value
Original Concept by Richard J.Maybury
Math Calculations Contributed by Brian C. Williams
(for ages 15 and up)

Inflation is a hidden tax. Understanding it is very important for the wise management of your investments, as well as planning for your future.

Suppose that in the year 2000 you put $100,000 into an investment and then five years later you sell it for $150,000. You made a profit of $50,000, right?

Probably not. A dollar in the year 2005 is unlikely to be worth as much as a dollar in the year 2000. A way to calculate the real value of an investment is to use a measure of the effects of inflation. As an example, to find your investment's true performance, I will use the federal government's Consumer Price Index (CPI). You can find the CPI on the Internet at the web site of the Federal Reserve Bank of St. Louis (http://www.stlouisfed.org/).

When reading the following example, don't feel intimidated by what may appear to be complex explanations and equations. In geometry an equation or formula represents a concept or idea. For example, the area of a rectangle is equal to its length times its width. This is most often represented as the equation $A = L \times W$ where A denotes the area of a rectangle, L denotes the length and W denotes the width.

In our example, and the exercises that follow, each step deals with a specific economic concept or idea about the effects of inflation and the federal government's CPI. Each idea is then represented in the form of an equation (formula). After solving for a specific value in each step you will have an overall understanding of the result you are trying to find—the true performance of an investment. The arithmetic you will use in each step is basic, but the final results will be amazing. Have fun.

To get a revealing picture of what is happening to your investment dollars, let's evaluate the true performance of your $100,000 investment if you sell it for $150,000 in the year 2005 in terms of a year 2000 dollar.

In our example and all exercises, assume the following:

Let $\mathbf{CPI}_i$ denote the government's CPI at the time the investment is made.

Let $\mathbf{CPI}_s$ denote the government's estimated CPI at the time you sell the investment.

Let $\mathbf{I}_i$ denote the dollar amount of your initial investment.

Let $\mathbf{I}_s$ denote the dollar amount of your investment at the time of sale.

Note: The Greek letter, Δ (delta) represents the difference between quantities.

Example

To find an investment's true performance, proceed as follows: (In this example, Year 2000 CPI = 200; Year 2005 CPI=300; Investment = $100,000. Selling Price =$150,000.)

1. **Calculate** the change in the CPI over 5 years:
    The change in the CPI over a given period of time is equal to the CPI at the time the investment is sold (CPI_s) minus the CPI at the time the investment is initially made (CPI_i).
    Let ΔCPI equal the change in the CPI over a given period of time.
    $$\Delta CPI = CPI_s - CPI_i$$
    $$\Delta CPI = 300\text{-}200$$
    $$\Delta CPI = \textbf{100 points}$$
    Therefore, the change in the government's CPI over 5 years is equal to a 100 point increase.

2. **Calculate** the percent change in the CPI over 5 years:
    The percent change in the CPI over a given period of time is equal to the change in the CPI (Δ **CPI**) divided by the CPI at the time of the investment (CPI_i).
    Let $\Delta CPI_\%$ denote the percent change in the CPI over time.
    $$\Delta CPI_\% = \Delta CPI \div CPI_i$$
    $$\Delta CPI_\% = 100 \div 200$$
    $$\Delta CPI_\% = .5 = \textbf{50\%}$$
    Therefore, the percent change in the government's CPI over 5 years is approximately equal to a 50% increase.

3. **Calculate** the value of a dollar in the year 2005 as a percent of the value of a dollar in the year 2000:
    The percent change in the value of a dollar is equal to the CPI at the time of the investment (CPI_i), divided by the CPI at the time the investment is sold (CPI_s).
    Let $\Delta D_\%$ denote the percent change in the value of a dollar over a given period of time.
    $$\Delta D_\% = CPI_i \div CPI_s$$
    $$\Delta D_\% = 200 \div 300$$
    $$\Delta D_\% = \textbf{.667} \text{ (rounded)} = \textbf{66.7\%}$$
    Therefore, the value of a dollar in the year 2005 is 66.7% of a year 2000 dollar. (A dollar in the year 2005 would have the value of 66.7¢ in the year 2000.)

4. **Calculate** the relative value of your investment when you sell it in the year 2005 in terms of the value of a dollar in the year 2000:
    The relative value of the selling price of your investment in terms of a dollar at the time the investment was made is equal to the percent change in the value of a dollar $(\Delta D_\%)$ times the dollar amount of the selling price of your investment (I_s).
    Let V_r denote the relative value of the selling price of your investment.
    $$V_r = \Delta D_\% \times I_s$$
    $$V_r = 66.7\% \times \$150,000 = .667 \times \$150,000$$
    $$V_r = \textbf{\$100,050}$$
    Therefore, the $100,000 investment that you made in the year 2000 and sold for $150,000 in the year 2005 is only worth $100,050 in terms of year 2000 dollars.

Your apparent $50,000 profit does not exist. In the year 2005, $150,000 will only have the value of $100,050 in year 2000 dollars. The difference between the selling price of your investment in the year 2005 and its value in terms of year 2000 dollars is a hidden tax the government has taken from you through inflation. The amount of value you lost is the amount the government gained by printing and spending new dollars. It gets worse. Your nonexistent $50,000 will be taxed when you sell your investment.

Now, to find your investment's true performance over a given period of time, calculate the following: For this example, assume the tax rate in the year 2005 equals 25%.

5. **Calculate** the gain (or loss) on your investment:
    The gain (or loss) on an investment is equal to the investment selling price (I_s) minus the initial investment amount (I_i).
    Let **G** denote gain at the time of sale.
    $$G = I_s - I_i$$
    $$G = \$150,000 - \$100,000$$
    $$\mathbf{G = \$50,000}$$
    Therefore, the gain on your $100,000 investment is $50,000.

6. **Calculate** the amount of tax you owe at the time you sell your investment in 2005:
    The tax owed is equal to the gain **(G)** times the tax rate at the time you sell.
    Let **T** denote tax owed at the time of sale.
    Let T_r denote the tax rate at the time of sale.
    $$T = T_r \times G$$
    $$T = 25\% \times \$50,000 = .25 \times \$50,000$$
    $$\mathbf{T = \$12,500}$$
    Therefore, you will owe $12,500 in taxes when you sell your investment in the year 2005.

7. **Calculate** the post tax amount of your investment in terms of year 2005 dollars:
    Let **N** denote the post tax dollar amount of your investment.
    $$N = I_s - T$$
    $$N = \$150,000 - \$12,500$$
    $$\mathbf{N = \$137,500}$$
    Therefore, of the $150,000 you sold your investment for in the year 2005, you only have $137,500 left after you pay taxes.

8. **Calculate** your post tax investment value in terms of year 2000 dollars:
    Your post tax investment value in terms of year 2000 dollars is equal to the post tax amount of your investment **(N)** times the percent change in the value of a dollar $(\Delta D_\%)$.
    Let **Q** denote your post tax investment value in terms of year 2000 dollars.
    $$Q = N \times \Delta D_\%$$
    $$Q = \$137,500 \times 66.7\% = \$137,500 \times .667$$
    $$\mathbf{Q = \$91,712}$$
    Therefore, in terms of year 2000 dollars the post tax value of your $100,000 investment which you sold for $150,000 in the year 2005 is $91,712.

9.   **Calculate** your investment's true performance:
     Your investment's true performance is equal to your post tax investment value (**Q**) minus your initial investment (**I$_i$**).
     Let **TP** denote the investment's true performance.

     TP = Q – I$_i$
     TP = $91,712 - $100,000
     TP = -$8,288

     Therefore, your investment's true performance is a **loss of $8,288.**

In other words, when you calculate your investment's true performance, you realize that hidden and unhidden taxes have hit you so hard that what at first glance appeared to be a profit of $50,000 is, in fact, a loss of $8,288.

When saving for something (perhaps to get married, a baby, college, retirement, or buying a house) you must plan for inflation. You must plan to save more than you would if there were no inflation. Otherwise you will end up with less than you need and will be sorely tempted to go deeply into debt, which is what millions end up doing.

How much more should you save? It is hard to say because government officials will decide how much they will inflate and how much they will tax you, and they change their minds continually.

Estimate the future cost of whatever you are saving for, then add an increase of at least 10% per year. This is a good starting point, but if you can save more, do it; the behavior of government officials is not predictable.

Here are more exercises to help you hone your skill in judging the effects of inflation.

Incidentally, if you have never run into exercises like this before, this is not an accident. There are people who do not want you to understand what is happening to you.

Exercises

Find the following for each exercise.
1)   The change in the CPI (**Δ CPI**).
2)   The percent change in the CPI (**Δ CPI$_\%$**).
3)   The value of a dollar in the year your investment is sold
     as a percent of the value of a dollar in the year of your initial investment (**Δ D$_\%$**).
4)   The value of your investment when you sell it in terms of the value of a dollar in the year of your initial investment (**V$_r$**).
5)   The gain or loss on your investment (**G**).
6)   The amount of tax you owe at the time you sell your investment (**T**).
7)   The dollar amount of your investment after taxes (**N**).
8)   Your post tax investment value in terms of a dollar in the year of your initial investment (**Q**).
9)   Your investment's true performance (**TP**).

For all the exercises assume the year 2000 CPI is equal to 200. Solutions and answers can be found on page 102. (Round to the nearest whole dollar.)

Group One Exercises

A. **Initial investment** in the year 2000: $78,000.
   Selling price in the year 2005: $98,000.
   Year 2005 CPI: 288.
   Tax rate in the year 2005: 33%

B. **Initial investment** in the year 2000: $188,500.
   Selling price in the year 2005: $221,250.
   Year 2005 CPI: 242.
   Tax rate in the year 2005: 24%.

C. **Initial investment** in the year 2000: $105,000.
   Selling price in the year 2005: $125,000.
   Year 2005 CPI: 200.
   Tax rate in the year 2005: 24%.

D. **Initial investment** in the year 2000: $100,000.
   Selling price in the year 2005: $200,000.
   Year 2005 CPI: 200.
   Tax rate in the year 2005: 5%.

Group Two Exercises

E. **Original investment** in the year 2000: $78,000.
   Selling price in the year 2005: $98,000.
   Year 2005 CPI: 288.
   Tax rate in the year 2005: 5%.

F. **Original investment** in the year 2000: $78,000.
   Selling price in the year 2005: $98,000.
   Year 2005 CPI: 288.
   Tax rate in the year 2005: 50%.

G. **Original investment** in the year 2000: $188.500.
   Selling price in the year 2005: $221,250.
   Year 2005 CPI: 300.
   Tax rate in the year 2005: 24%.

H. **Original investment** in the year 2000: $188.500.
   Selling price in the year 2005: $221,250.
   Year 2005 CPI: 400.
   Tax rate in the year 2005: 24%.

Chapter 4: Dollars, Money, and Legal Tender

Define

1.   Dollar:

2.   Money:

3.   Coin:

4.   Hallmark:

5.   Banknote:

6.   Legal tender law:

7.   Fiat money:

Short Answer/Fill-in/True or False

8.   What characteristics must good money have?

9.   Throughout the centuries what two metals have had the characteristics of good money?

10. What other items have been used as money throughout the centuries?

11. Why were coins invented?

12. How did "dollar" get its name?

13. What are silver certificates?

14. Did silver certificates have legal tender statements? Explain your answer.

15. What has replaced the Silver Certificate and what is its impact on the value of U.S. currency?

16. What gives Federal Reserve Notes their value?

17. What happens if someone owes you money and you refuse to accept Federal Reserve Notes in payment of the debt?

18. What is the significance of Article 1, Section 10 of the U.S. Constitution in relation to the legal tender law?

19. By 2009, according to the government's own Consumer Price Index, the Federal Reserve dollar had lost _____% of the value it had in 1914.

20. When did gold and silver coins stop circulating in the United States?

21. How did the legal system affect the economy relative to the laws concerning the circulation of gold and silver, and the legal tender law?

Discussion/Essay/Assignment

22. When you were very young did you trade items with your friends? Usually when we talk about trading we think of exchanging one product for another. When we talk about buying or purchasing, we think of exchanging a product for coins or currency. Young children don't always have ready cash available, so they often resort to trading items they possess in exchange for items someone else possesses. Not having any, or little, notion about the cash value of an item, it is not unusual to hear stories of young children who have traded a $10 item for a $0.50 item. Usually when this happens, the parent of the child who "got the short end of the stick" steps in and calls the trade null and void. However, by intervening, the parent is causing a child to "not do what he or she has agreed to do."

    The better approach would be to anticipate that a child might want to trade with friends and plan a discussion about this—before a trade takes place. A parent can explain that until the young consumer can understand the cash value of items, the youngster should first consult with a parent before agreeing to the terms of any trade or outright cash sale. If the child fails to do this, then the child must accept any consequences of the trade, which can be a good lesson as well. (Review the article on page 37: *Free Market: Elementary, My Child*). In either case, the child is learning to take responsibility for his or her actions. This is a fundamental principle in free markets. (This raises additional points, which will be discussed in the study guide for Richard J. Maybury's book WHATEVER HAPPENED TO JUSTICE? which emphasizes property, ownership, and contract.)

    When the child begins to receive money for services or chores, this is a good time to help the child begin to realize that money is a measurement for services rendered for a set period of time worked. Then it becomes easier to explain what the value of an item is relative to the number of hours a child must work to exchange his labor (measured in money) for that item.

For Further Reading

23. ROUND AND ROUND THE MONEY GOES by Melvin and Gilda Berger (for ages 5-9) published by Ideals Childrens Books. [For discussion: What information is missing from ROUND AND ROUND THE MONEY GOES that Richard Maybury (Uncle Eric) talks about in the chapter *Dollars, Money, and Legal Tender*?]

24. *Eternal Love* by Lawrence Noonan (for ages 14 and up) in ECONOMICS: A FREE MARKET READER, published by Bluestocking Press, phone: 800-959-8586, web site: www. BluestockingPress.com. [For discussion: What might be considered the hallmark of the platinum item made by Charles Akin? How does this story illustrate Richard Maybury's (Uncle Eric's) explanation of what constitutes a real coin?]

25. *Back to Gold* by Henry Hazlitt (for ages 14 an up) in ECONOMICS: A FREE MARKET READER, published by Bluestocking Press, phone: 800-959-8586, web site: www. BluestockingPress.com.

26. *Not Worth a Continental* by Pelatiah Webster (for ages 16 and up) (originally published December 13, 1780), reprinted in ECONOMICS: A FREE MARKET READER, published by Bluestocking Press, phone: 800-959-8586, web site: www.BluestockingPress.com.

27. *The Gold Problem* by Ludwig von Mises (for ages 16 and up) in ECONOMICS: A FREE MARKET READER, published by Bluestocking Press, phone: 800-959-8586, web site: www. BluestockingPress.com.

28. *Ideas on Liberty* by F.A. Harper (for ages 15 and up). See boxed article below.

Ideas on Liberty
by F. A. Harper
(for ages 15 and up)

Intellectual and moral guidance, voluntarily accepted by the follower, is no violation of liberty; it is, in fact, a main purpose of liberty so that the blind are free to follow those who can see. The danger is that in the absence of liberty the blind may become authorized to lead those who can see—by a chain around their necks!

The terrific urge to prevent another person from making a "mistake" must be resisted if liberty is to be preserved. The "protective spirit" that leads a fond parent to prohibit his child from acquiring mature judgments, as he substitutes his own opinions for those of the child, leads the dictator to act as he does in "protecting" his political children. There is no possible way to allow a person to be right without also allowing him to be wrong. The only way to avoid responsibility for another's mistakes is to allow him the full glory and reward of being right, as well as the full dishonor and penalty of being wrong. Only in this way can one person isolate himself from the mistakes of another, whether it be a Stalin or a neighbor.

Reprinted with permission of the Foundation for Economic Education, 30 S. Broadway, Irvington-on-Hudson, New York 10533, web address: http://fee.org

Chapter 5: Revolutions, Elections, and Printing Presses

Define
1. Revolution:

Short Answer/Fill-in/True or False

2. According to Mr. Maybury (Uncle Eric), all governments inflate. What are the reasons for inflating in a dictatorship?

3. What are the reasons for inflating in a democracy?

4. Besides using money to inflate, how else do modern politicians inflate?

Discussion/Essay/Assignment

5. In an election year, whether it's national, state or local, make a list of what each politician promises the electorate (the voting public). How much of what is promised to the electorate will require funding (money) to carry out? From where will the funds come? How will the government acquire the money to fund the programs promised by the politician?

For Further Reading

6. *Not Yours to Give* by David Crockett (for ages 14 and up) in ECONOMICS: A FREE MARKET READER, published by Bluestocking Press, phone: 800-959-8586, web site: www. BluestockingPress.com.

7. Try to locate a copy of Harry Browne's 1971 book *How You Can Profit from the Coming Devaluation* (for ages 14 and up). It is currently out of print, so try to find it in your library. If your library doesn't have it, ask if they can borrow it from another library. A charge might be involved in this. Otherwise, try a book search service. Read the first 100 pages for a clear explanation of how banks and the Federal Reserve are used to inflate.

Big Mac Index

Discussion/Essay/Assignment

1. Compare the value of the U.S. dollar relative to other currencies. Visit the following online site: www.economist.com/markets/bigmac/index.cfm or conduct an internet search for "Big Mac Index" and read the article "Burgernomics: When the Chips Are Down." Also read current articles that might be posted at this site on this topic. Next, visit the online site: www.measuringworth.com/uscompare for measuring different foreign currency values against the U.S. dollar. What are your conclusions about the value of the U.S. dollar relative to foreign currencies?

Chapter 6: Wages, Prices, Spirals, and Controls

Short Answer/Fill-in/True or False

1.   Is the wage/price spiral a cause of inflation or a result of inflation?

2.   True or False: Large increases in the supply of money are always followed by increases in wages and prices.

3.   True or False: Large decreases in the supply of money are always followed by a fall in wages and prices.

4.   Is there ever an exception to #3 above? Explain.

5.   True or False: With a few exceptions, there has never been a case where wages and prices rose rapidly without someone creating a lot of money.

Discussion/Essay/Assignment

6.   If the supply of money does not change, then the only way for one person to have more money is for someone else to have less. Find out if your parents budget their household income. If so, what happens if a child in the family needs, for example, orthodontic work? From where does the money come, if salary/wages remain constant? Consumers, like your parents, can spend no more than they earn without going into debt. In contrast, government can place more money into circulation to pay for what it wants.

7.   People's wants, needs, and desires are what move life, and the economy is no exception. For example, suppose you baby sit for money and you charge $2.00/hr to babysit. Suddenly the government passes a law that says you may charge no more than $2.00/hr to babysit. Someone has six children and wants you to babysit all of them for $2.00/hr. Will you do this? Will you refuse the job? Will you take a more attractive job in which you have only one child to babysit? Will this type of government policy stimulate the economy or stifle it? Explain.

8.   Let's look at another example. You are a landlord of an apartment building. Government passes a law that says you may not raise the rent. As time passes, your cost to maintain your building increases, but you are unable to collect additional rent because it's against the law. What can you do? Will someone else want to buy your building? Why or why not?

9.   Controls and confiscation of one's productivity curb incentive to produce, just as the incentive for profit encourages economic production. For example, the early colonies in America were settled on communist principles: from each according to his ability to each according to his need. (It wasn't until this concept failed and the colonies turned to a free market system that they began to prosper.) Can you recall any situations where this principle is applied in families today? Have you ever observed a parent who expected an

older child to do more than a younger child, just because the older child was more capable? Did the children in the situation benefit equally? How is this example similar or different from the communist principle? (Review the following articles that appear earlier in this study guide:

    1) *Letter to His Grandson* (page 24)

    2) *I, Pencil* (page 20)

    3) *The Cow in the Apartment* (page 26)

For Further Reading

10. *A Job for All* by Percy L. Greaves, Jr. (for ages 14 and up) in ECONOMICS: A FREE MARKET READER, published by Bluestocking Press, phone: 800-959-8586, web site: www.BluestockingPress.com. [How does this article exemplify Mr. Maybury's (Uncle Eric's) explanations in the chapter *Wages, Prices, Spirals and Controls?*]

11. *Competition, Monopoly and the Role of Government* by Sylvester Petro (for ages 14 and up) in ECONOMICS: A FREE MARKET READER, published by Bluestocking Press, phone: 800-959-8586, web site: www.BluestockingPress.com. [Petro includes an excerpt from Mark Twain's LIFE ON THE MISSISSIPPI about the river steamboat pilots forming an association. What was the result of their union on the profitability of the steamboat industry?

12. *Dear Mr. Ag Secretary* (see next page), author unknown, (for ages 10 and up), and *A Lesson in Socialism* (page 63) by Thomas J. Shelly (for ages 15 and up). [Explain why you agree or disagree with Mr. Shelly's statement: "Socialism—even in a democracy—will eventually result in a living-death for all except the 'authorities' and a few of their favorite lackeys."]

The following letter is excellent discussion material about the subject of government intervention in the economy. The author is unknown.

Dear Mr. Ag Secretary
(for ages 10 and up)

Dear Mr. Ag Secretary:

My friend Mort Wilson received a check for $1,000 from the government for not raising hogs. So I want to get into the "not raising hogs" business next year. What I want to know is, in your opinion, what is the best type of farm to not raise hogs on, and what is the best breed of hogs not to raise?

If I get $1,000 for not raising 50 hogs, will I get $2,000 for not raising 100 hogs? I plan to operate on a small scale at first, holding myself down to about 4,000 "not raised" hogs, which will give me $80,000 income the first year. Then I can afford an airplane.

Now, another thing: These hogs I will not raise will not eat 100,000 bushels of corn. I understand that you also pay farmers for not raising corn and wheat. Will I qualify for payments for not raising wheat and corn not to feed the 4,000 hogs I am not going to raise?

I am also considering not milking cows, so please send me information on that, too.

In view of these circumstances, I understand that the government will consider me unemployed, so I plan to file for unemployment and food stamps.

Be assured that you will have my vote in the coming elections.

Patriotically yours,

A. Prospective Farmer
Kansas

A Lesson In Socialism
by Thomas J. Shelly
(for ages 15 and up)

As a teacher in the public schools, I find that the socialist-communist idea of taking "from each according to his ability," and giving "to each according to his need" is now generally accepted without question by most of our pupils. In an effort to explain the fallacy in this theory, I sometimes try this approach with my pupils:

When one of the brighter or harder-working pupils makes a grade of 95 on a test, I suggest that I take away 20 points and give them to a student who has made only 55 points on his test. Thus each would contribute according to his ability and—since both would have a passing mark—each would receive according to his need. After I have juggled the grades of all the other pupils in this fashion, the result is usually a "common ownership" grade of between 75 and 80—the minimum needed for passing, or for survival. Then I speculate with the pupils as to the probable results if I actually used the socialistic theory for grading papers.

First, the highly productive pupils—and they are always a minority in school as well as in life—would soon lose all incentive for producing. Why strive to make a high grade if part of it is taken from you by "authority" and given to someone else?

Second, the less productive pupils—a majority in school as elsewhere—would, for a time, be relieved of the necessity to study or to produce. This socialist-communist system would continue until the high producers had sunk—or had been driven down—to the level of the low producers. At that point, in order for anyone to survive, the "authority" would have no alternative but to begin a system of compulsory labor and punishments against even the low producers. They, of course, would then complain bitterly, but without understanding.

Finally I return the discussion to the ideas of freedom and enterprise—the market economy—where each person has freedom of choice and is responsible for his own decisions and welfare.

Gratifyingly enough, most of my pupils then understand what I mean when I explain that socialism—even in a democracy—will eventually result in a living-death for all except the "authorities" and a few of their favorite lackeys.

Reprinted with permission of the Foundation for Economic Education, 30 S. Broadway, Irvington-on-Hudson, New York 10533, web address: http://fee.org

Chapter 7: Wallpaper, Wheelbarrows, and Recessions

Define

1. Runaway inflation:

2. Depression:

3. Recession:

4. Deflation:

Short Answer/Fill-in/True or False

5. What is the business cycle and what causes it?

For Research (Discuss findings or write an essay):

6. Refer to the Economic Timetable. List the years in which depressions, recessions, and inflations occurred.

For Further Reading

7. For a further explanation of the business cycle read Richard J. Maybury's "Uncle Eric" book THE CLIPPER SHIP STRATEGY, the second sequel to WHATEVER HAPPENED TO PENNY CANDY? It gives a detailed explanation of government's injections of money into the economy and how this manipulation of the money supply affects business, careers, and investments. For ages 14 and up, published by Bluestocking Press, phone: 800-959-8586, web site: www. BluestockingPress.com

Chapter 8: Fast Money

Define

1. Velocity:

2. Demand for money:

Short Answer/Fill-in/True or False

3. Why would people want to trade away their money quickly?

4. True or False: If the demand for money falls, money changes hands faster.

5. What is the term for the speed at which money changes hands?

6.   In order for velocity to fall, the demand for money must _____.

7.   What are the three stages of inflation?

8.   When does runaway inflation end?

9.   What keeps velocity under control?

10.   What two things can cause people to change their spending habits enough to change velocity? Give examples of each.

11.   Do inflations have to follow the 1, 2, 3 stages described in "Fast Money"? Explain. List examples from history to support your answer.

Discussion/Essay/Assignment

12.   If bad money is driven out of circulation, would precious metals coins be accepted in exchange for goods and services? Explain. Would it be a good idea to always keep a certain amount of gold and silver in the form of coins? Explain. If you kept gold and silver would it be for investment, or as a form of insurance? Explain.

For Further Reading

13.   Read the first sequel to WHATEVER HAPPENED TO PENNY CANDY? titled THE MONEY MYSTERY by Richard J. Maybury (for ages 14 and up), which is a further explanation of velocity, published by Bluestocking Press, web site: www.BluestockingPress.com

14.   ROUND AND ROUND THE MONEY GOES by Melvin and Gilda Berger (for ages 5-9), published by Ideals Childrens Books. [What is the velocity of the dollar as of the first three pages?]

15.   THE GO-AROUND DOLLAR by Barbara Johnston Adams (for ages 6-9) published by Simon and Schuster. [What is the velocity of the dollar Matt finds in the story?]

History Repeats

Discussion/Essay/Assignment

1.   During the 1920s, investors spent their money on _____.

2.   During the 1990s, investors spent their money on _____.

3.   When the bubble of the 1990s burst, where was much of the newly created money invested?

Chapter 9: Getting Rich Quick

Define

1.   Business cycle:

Short Answer/Fill-in/True or False

2.   List an example of America's boom-and-bust cycle. Explain your reasons for your choice.

For Further Reading

3.   Richard Maybury (Uncle Eric) says to "stay away from get-rich-quick fads—or be very careful. Learn everything there is to know about your investments." The following article, *Investment Survival in Today's Tough World* is very important. It has been reprinted with the permission of the author, Richard Russell, and addresses the subject of compound interest.

4.   For an excellent children's folktale that can help youngsters understand compounding of interest, through the concept of doubling, read ONE GRAIN OF RICE: A MATHEMATICAL FOLK TALE by Demi (for ages 6-10) published by Scholastic Press.

5.   Richard J. Maybury encourages investing in yourself by investing in your own business. For further reading about entrepreneurship and business sense for kids, read: 1) COMMON SENSE BUSINESS FOR KIDS by Kathryn Daniels (for ages 13 through 15), published by Bluestocking Press, phone: 800-959-8586, web site: www.BluestockingPress.com; 2) BETTER THAN A LEMONADE STAND by Daryl Bernstein (for ages 9 through 12), published by Beyond Words Publishing; 3) CAPITALISM FOR KIDS by Karl Hess (for ages 13 through 17), published by Bluestocking Press; and 4) THE YOUNG ENTREPRENEURS GUIDE TO STARTING AND RUNNING A BUSINESS by Steve Mariotti (for ages 14 and up), published by Random House.

6.   For further reading about Business Cycle Management, read the Uncle Eric book THE CLIPPER SHIP STRATEGY by Richard J. Maybury (for ages 14 and up), published by Bluestocking Press, phone: 800-959-8586, web site: www.BluestockingPress.com.

7.   For further reading about the Great Depression, read Murray Rothbard's book AMERICA'S GREAT DEPRESSION (for ages 15 and up), available through www.mises.org.

To View

8.   KIDCO directed by Ronald F. Maxwell, Playhouse Video, 1984, 20th Century Fox Film Corp. Comedy about siblings starting a successful manure business. Based on a true-life story. Rated PG, however, parents are encouraged to preview this film.

Read the article starting on the next page.
It could be worth over $900,000 to you!

Investment Survival in Today's Tough World
by Richard Russell
(for ages 12 and up)

Reprinted from July 17, 1996 issue of Dow Theory Letters,
with the permission of Richard Russell publisher, Dow Theory Letters, La Jolla, CA.

MAKING MONEY: The most popular piece I've published in 38 years of writing these Letters was entitled, "Rich Man, Poor Man." I last ran this piece back in June of 1990. Since then I have had dozens of requests to run this piece again or for permission to reprint it for various business organizations. When I ran the piece in '90 I added a few items, and I want to do that again. So let's call the current article, simply "Investment Survival in Today's Tough World."

Here in 1996 I'm flooded with advertisements and mailings all telling me "how I can make a killing in the stock market." Every other magazine features a cover story which tells me what mutual funds I should buy. Newspapers, TV and radio feature "the best mutual funds to retire on." It's a veritable blizzard of information — "how you and I can make it, and make it big, in the stock market."

Now I'm not ridiculing these ads and mailings and info-mercials — the fact is that many of them are cleverly written and fascinating. But I wonder how much use they are to the average investor. And I ask myself, "How many of the writers and advisors who wrote these pieces have actually made any 'real money' for themselves?" My answer is, "Not many," and I know this for a fact, because I know a great many of the advisors.

Reprinted from July 17, 1996 issue of *Dow Theory Letters,* with the permission of Richard Russell publisher, Dow Theory Letters, La Jolla, CA.

Making money entails a lot more than predicting which way the stock or bond markets are heading or trying to figure which stock or fund will double over the next few years. For the great majority of investors, making money requires a plan, self-discipline and desire. I say, "for the great majority of people" because if you're a Steven Spielberg or a Bill Gates you don't have to know about the Dow or the markets or about yields or price/earnings ratios. You're a phenomenon in your own field, and you're going to make big money as a by-product of your talent and ability. But this kind of genius is rare.

For the average investor, you and me, we're not geniuses so we have to have a **financial plan**. In view of this, I offer below a few items that we must be aware of if we are serious about making money.

RULE 1: COMPOUNDING: One of the most important lessons for living in the modern world is that to survive you've got to have money. But to live (survive) *happily*, you must have love, health (mental and physical), freedom, intellectual stimulation — and money. When I taught my kids about money, the first thing I taught them was the use of the "money bible." What's the money bible? Simple, it's a volume of the *compounding interest tables*.

Compounding is the royal road to riches. Compounding is the safe road, the sure road, and fortunately, anybody can do it. To compound successfully you need the following: **perseverance** in order to keep you firmly on the savings path.

You need **intelligence** in order to understand what you are doing and why. And you need a **knowledge** of the mathematics tables in order to comprehend the amazing rewards that will come to you if you faithfully follow the compounding road. And, of course, you need **time**, time to allow the power of compounding to work for you. Remember, compounding *only works through time*.

But there are two catches in the compounding process. The first is obvious—compounding may involve sacrifice (you can't spend it and still save it). Second, compounding is boring—b-o-r-i-n-g. Or I should say it's boring until (after seven or eight years) the money starts to pour in. Then, believe me, compounding becomes very interesting. In fact, it becomes downright fascinating!

In order to emphasize the power of compounding, I am including this extraordinary study, courtesy of *Market Logic*, of Ft. Lauderdale, FL 33306. In this study we assume that investor (B) opens an IRA at age 19. For seven consecutive periods he puts $2,000 in his IRA at an average growth rate of 10% (7% interest plus growth). After seven years this fellow makes NO MORE contributions—he's finished.

	Investor A		Investor B	
Age	Contri-bution	Year-End Value	Contri-bution	Year-End Value
8	0	0	0	0
9	0	0	0	0
10	0	0	0	0
11	0	0	0	0
12	0	0	0	0
13	0	0	0	0
14	0	0	0	0
15	0	0	0	0
16	0	0	0	0
17	0	0	0	0
18	0	0	0	0
19	0	0	2,000	2,200
20	0	0	2,000	4,620
21	0	0	2,000	7,282
22	0	0	2,000	10,210
23	0	0	2,000	13,431
24	0	0	2,000	16,974
25	0	0	2,000	20,872
26	2,000	2,200	0	22,959
27	2,000	4,620	0	25,255
28	2,000	7,282	0	27,780
29	2,000	10,210	0	30,558
30	2,000	13,431	0	33,614
31	2,000	16,974	0	36,976
32	2,000	20,872	0	40,673
33	2,000	25,159	0	44,741
34	2,000	29,875	0	49,215
35	2,000	35,062	0	54,136
36	2,000	40,769	0	59,550
37	2,000	47,045	0	65,505
38	2,000	53,950	0	72,055
39	2,000	61,545	0	79,261
40	2,000	69,899	0	87,187
41	2,000	79,089	0	95,905
42	2,000	89,198	0	105,496
43	2,000	100,318	0	116,045
44	2,000	112,550	0	127,650
45	2,000	126,005	0	140,415
46	2,000	140,805	0	154,456
47	2,000	157,086	0	169,902
48	2,000	174,995	0	186,892
49	2,000	194,694	0	205,581
50	2,000	216,364	0	226,140
51	2,000	240,200	0	248,754
52	2,000	266,420	0	273,629
53	2,000	295,262	0	300,992
54	2,000	326,988	0	331,091
55	2,000	361,887	0	364,200
56	2,000	400,276	0	400,620
57	2,000	442,503	0	440,682
58	2,000	488,953	0	484,750
59	2,000	540,049	0	533,225
60	2,000	596,254	0	586,548
61	2,000	658,079	0	645,203
62	2,000	726,087	0	709,723
63	2,000	800,896	0	780,695
64	2,000	883,185	0	858,765
65	2,000	973,704	0	944,641
Less Total Invested:		(80,000)		(14,000)
Equals Net Earnings:		$893,704		$930,641
Money Grew:		11-fold		66-fold

A second investor (A) makes no contributions until age 26 (this is the age when investor B was finished with his contributions). Then A continues faithfully to contribute $2,000 every year until he's 65 (at the same theoretical 10% rate).

Now study the incredible results. B, who made his contributions earlier and who made only seven contributions, ends up with MORE money than A, who made 40 contributions but at a LATER TIME. The difference in the two is that *B had seven more early years of compounding than A*. Those seven early years were worth more than all of A's 33 additional contributions.

This is a study that I suggest you show to your kids. It's a study I've lived by, and I can tell you, "It works." You can work your compounding with muni-bonds, with a good money market fund, with T-bills or say with five-year T-notes.

RULE 2: DON'T LOSE MONEY: This may sound naive, but believe me it isn't. If you want to be wealthy, you must not lose money, or I should say must not lose BIG money. Absurd rule, silly rule? Maybe, but MOST PEOPLE LOSE MONEY in disastrous investments, gambling, rotten business deals, greed, poor timing. Yes, after almost five decades of investing and talking to investors, I can tell you that most people definitely DO lose money, lose big time—in the stock market, in options and futures, in real estate, in bad loans, in mindless gambling, and in their own business.

RULE 3: RICH MAN, POOR MAN: In the investment world the wealthy investor has one major advantage over the little guy, the stock market amateur and the neophyte trader. The advantage that the wealthy investor enjoys is that HE DOESN'T NEED THE MARKETS. I can't begin to tell you what a difference that makes, both in one's mental attitude and in the way one actually handles one's money.

The wealthy investor doesn't need the markets, because **he already has all the income he needs.** He has money coming in via bonds, T-bills, money market funds, stocks and real estate. In other words, the wealthy investor *never feels pressured* to "make money" in the market.

The wealthy investor tends to be an expert on **values**. When bonds are cheap and bond yields are irresistibly high, he buys bonds. When stocks are on the bargain table and stock yields are attractive, he buys stocks. When real estate is a great value, he buys real estate. When great art or fine jewelry or gold is on the "give away" table, he buys art or diamonds or gold. In other words, the wealthy investor puts his money where the great values are.

And if no outstanding values are available, the wealthy investor waits. He can afford to wait. He has money coming in daily, weekly, monthly. The wealthy investor knows what he is looking for, and he doesn't mind waiting months or even years for his next investment (they call that **patience**).

But what about the little guy? This fellow always feels pressured to "make money." And in return he's always pressuring the market to "do something" for him. But sadly, the market isn't interested. When the little guy isn't buying stocks offering 1% or 2% yields, he's off to Las Vegas or Atlantic City trying to beat the house at roulette. Or he's spending 20 bucks a week on lottery tickets, or he's "investing" in some crackpot scheme that his neighbor told him about (in strictest confidence, of course).

And because the little guy is trying to force the market to do something for him, he's a guaranteed loser. The little guy doesn't understand values so he constantly overpays. He doesn't comprehend the power of compounding, and he doesn't understand money. He's never heard the adage, *"He who understands interest—earns it.*

He who doesn't understand interest—pays it." The little guy is the typical American, and he's deeply in debt.

The little guy is in hock up to his ears. As a result, he's always sweating—sweating to make payments on his house, his refrigerator, his car or his lawn mower. He's impatient, and he feels perpetually put upon. He tells himself that he has to make money—fast. And he dreams of those "big, juicy mega-bucks." In the end, the little guy wastes his money in the market, or he loses his money gambling, or he dribbles it away on senseless schemes. In short, this "money-nerd" spends his life dashing up the financial down-escalator.

But here's the ironic part of it. If, from the beginning, the little guy had adopted a strict policy of never spending more than he made, if he had taken his extra savings and compounded it in intelligent, income-producing securities, then in due time he'd have money coming in daily, weekly, monthly, just like the rich man. The little guy would have become a financial winner, instead of a pathetic loser.

RULE 4: VALUES: The only time the average investor should stray outside the basic compounding system is when a given market offers outstanding value. I judge an investment to be a great value when it offers (a) safety; (b) an attractive return; and (c) a good chance of appreciating in price. At all other times, the compounding route is safer and probably a lot more profitable, at least in the long run.

Reprinted from July 17, 1996 issue of *Dow Theory Letters,* with the permission of Richard Russell publisher, Dow Theory Letters, La Jolla, CA.

Chapter 10: The Boom and Bust Cycle

Define

1.   Stock:

Short Answer/Fill-in/True or False

2.   What is M2?

3.   How do we determine the "real" M2 money supply?

4.   What happens when the government slows the creation of real M2?

5.   What was the reason for the stock market crash of 1987?

For Research (Discuss findings or write an essay)**:**

6.   Refer to the Economic Timetable. What was M2 in February 1997? What is M2 today?

For Further Reading

7.   Read *Nine Myths About the Crash* by Murray N. Rothbard, next page, for ages 15 and up, which explains the myths surrounding the 1987 stock market crash.

Nine Myths About the Crash
by Murray N. Rothbard
(for ages 15 and up)

Ever since Black, or Meltdown, Monday October 19th, the public has been deluged with irrelevant and contradictory explanations and advice from politicians, economists, financiers, and assorted pundits.

Let's try to sort out and rebut some of the nonsense about the nature, causes, and remedies for the crash.

Myth One

It was not a crash, but a "correction."

Rubbish. The market was in a virtual crash state since it started turning down sharply from its all-time peak at the end of August. Meltdown Monday simply put the seal on a contraction process that had gone on since early September.

Myth Two

The crash occurred because stock prices had been "overvalued," and now the overvaluation has been cured.

This adds a philosophical fallacy to Myth #1. To say that stock prices fell because they had been overvalued is equivalent to the age-old fallacy of "explaining" why opium puts people to sleep by saying that it "has dormitive power." A definition has been magically transmuted into a "cause." By definition, if stock prices fall, this means that they had been previously overvalued. So what? This "explanation" tells you nothing about why they were overvalued or whether or not they are "over" or "under" valued now, or what in the world is going to happen next.

Myth Three

The crash came about because of computer trading, which in association with stock index futures, has made the stock market more volatile. Therefore computer trading and/or stock index futures, should be restricted/outlawed.

This is a variant of the scapegoat term "computer error" employed to get "people errors" off the hook. It is also a variant of the old Luddite fallacy of blaming modern technology for human error and taking a crowbar to wreck the new machines. People trade, and people program computers. Empirically, moreover, the "tape" was hours behind the action on Black Monday, and so computers played a minimal role. Stock index futures are an excellent new way for investors to hedge against stock price changes, and should be welcomed instead of fastened on—by its competitors in the old-line exchanges—to be tagged as the fall guy for the crash.

Blaming futures or computer trading is like shooting the messenger—the markets—that bring bad financial news. The acme of this reaction was the threat—and sometimes the reality—of forcibly shutting down the exchanges in a pitiful and futile attempt to hold back the news by destroying it. The Hong Kong exchange closed down for a week to try to stem the crash and, when it reopened, found that the ensuing crash was far worse as a result.

Myth Four

A major cause of the crash was the big trade deficit in the U.S.

Nonsense. There is nothing wrong with a trade deficit. In fact, there is no payment deficit at all. If U.S. imports are greater than exports, they must be paid for somehow, and the way they are paid is that foreigners invest in dollars, so that there is a capital inflow into the U.S. In that way, a big trade deficit results in a zero payment deficit.

Foreigners have been investing heavily in dollars—in Treasury deficits, in real estate, factories, etc.—for several years, and that's a good thing, since it enables Americans to enjoy a higher-valued dollar (and consequently cheaper imports) than would otherwise be the case.

But, say the advocates of Myth #4, the terrible thing is that the U.S. has, in recent years, become a debtor instead of a creditor nation. So what's wrong with that? The United States was in the same way a debtor nation from the beginning of the republic until World War I, and that was accompanied by the largest rate of economic and industrial growth and of rising living standards, in the history of mankind.

Myth Five

The budget deficit is a major cause of the crash, and we must work hard to reduce that deficit, either by cutting government spending, and/or by raising taxes.

The budget deficit is most unfortunate, and causes economic problems, but the stock market crash was not one of them. Just because something is bad policy doesn't mean that all economic ills are caused by it. Basically, the budget deficit is as irrelevant to the crash, as the even larger deficit was irrelevant to the pre-September 1987 stock market boom.

Raising taxes is now the favorite crash remedy of both liberal and conservative Keynesians. Here, one of the few good points in the original, or "classical," Keynesian view has been curiously

forgotten. How in the world can one cure a crash (or the coming recession), by raising taxes?

Raising taxes will clearly level a damaging blow to an economy already reeling from the crash. Increasing taxes to cure a crash was one of the major policies of the unlamented program of Herbert Hoover. Are we longing for a replay? The idea that a tax increase would "reassure" the market is straight out of Cloud Cuckoo-land.

Myth Six

The budget should be cut, but not by much, because much lower government spending would precipitate a recession.

Unfortunately, the way things are, we don't have to worry about a big cut in government spending. Such a cut would be marvelous, not only for its own sake, but because a slash in the budget would reduce the unproductive boondoggles of government spending, and therefore tip the social proportion of saving/consumption toward more saving and investment.

More saving/investment in relation to consumption is an Austrian remedy for easing a recession, and reducing the amount of corrective liquidation that the recession has to perform, in order to correct the malinvestments of the boom caused by the inflationary expansion of bank credit.

Myth Seven

What we need to offset the crash and stave off a recession is lots of monetary inflation (called by the euphemistic term "liquidity") and lower interest rates. Fed chairman Alan Greenspan did exactly the right thing by pumping in reserves right after the crash, and announcing that the Fed would assure plenty of liquidity for banks and for the entire market and the whole economy. (A position taken by every single variant of the conventional economic wisdom, from Keynesians to "free marketers.")

In this way, Greenspan and the federal government have proposed to cure the disease—the crash and future recession—by pouring into the economy more of the very virus (inflationary credit expansion) that caused the disease in the first place. Only in Cloud Cuckoo-land, to repeat, is the cure for inflation, more inflation.

To put it simply: the reason for the crash was the credit boom generated by the double-digit monetary expansion engineered by the Fed in the last several years. For a few years, as always happens in Phase I of an inflation, prices went up less than the monetary inflation. This, the typical euphoric phase of inflation, was the "Reagan miracle" of cheap and abundant money, accompanied by moderate price increases.

By 1986, the main factors that had offset the monetary inflation and kept prices relatively low (the unusually high dollar and the OPEC collapse) had worked their way through the price system and disappeared. The next inevitable step was the return and acceleration of price inflation; inflation rose from about 1% in 1986 to about 5% in 1987. As a result, with the market sensitive to and expecting eventual reacceleration of inflation, interest rates began to rise sharply in 1987. Once interest rates rose (which had little or nothing to do with the budget deficit), a stock market crash was inevitable. The previous stock market boom had been built on the shaky foundation of the low interest rates from 1982 on.

Myth Eight

The crash was precipitated by the Fed's unwise tight money policy from April 1987 on, after which the money supply was flat until the crash.

There is a point here, but a totally distorted one. A flat money supply for six months probably made a coming recession inevitable, and added to the stock market crash. But that tight money was a good thing nevertheless. No other school of economic thought but the Austrian understands that once an inflationary bank credit boom has been launched, a corrective recession is inevitable, and that the sooner it comes, the better.

The sooner a recession comes the fewer the unsound investments that the recession has to liquidate, and the sooner the recession will be over. The important point about a recession is for the government not to interfere, not to inflate, not to regulate, and to allow the recession to work its curative way as quickly as possible. Interfering with the recession, either by inflating or regulating, can only prolong the recession and make it worse, as in the 1930s. And yet the pundits, the economists of all schools, the politicians of both parties, rush heedless into the agreed-upon policies of: Inflate, and Regulate.

Myth Nine

Before the crash, the main danger was inflation, and the Fed was right to tighten credit. But since the crash, we have to shift gears, because recession is the major enemy, and therefore the Fed has to inflate, at least until price inflation accelerates rapidly.

This entire analysis, permeating the media and the Establishment, assumes that the great fact and the great lesson of the 1970s, and of the last two big recessions, never happened: i.e., inflationary recession. The 1970s have gone down the Orwellian memory hole, and the Establishment is back, once again, spouting the Keynesian Phillips Curve, perhaps the greatest single and most absurd error in modern economics.

The Phillips Curve assumes that the choice is always either more recession and unemployment, or more inflation. In reality, the Phillips Curve, if one wishes to speak in those terms, is in reverse: the choice is either more inflation and bigger recession, or none of either. The looming danger is another inflationary recession, and the Greenspan reaction indicates that it will be a whopper.

Reprinted from *The Free Market*, January 1988 issue, with permission of the Ludwig von Mises Institute, 518 West Magnolia Avenue, Auburn, AL 36832-4528, web address: mises.org

Chapter 11: How Much is a Trillion?

For Research

1. The 1993 printing of WHATEVER HAPPENED TO PENNY CANDY stated the federal debt was four trillion dollars. What is the federal debt today? What is each person's share of the debt today? (Divide debt by population.) [To find the current federal debt, conduct an internet search for U.S. National Debt Clock or U.S. Debt Clock. URLs change frequently, but at the time I write this this, current URLs are: DefeatTheDebt.com, www.brillig.com/debt_clock, and www.usdebtclock.org]

2. Refer to the Economic Timetable. Make a columnar report on a separate piece of paper. Label the first column "year," label the second column "federal debt," label the third column "population," and label the fourth column "per person share of the federal debt" (divide debt by population).   Record data for the following years: 1791, 1810, 1820, 1830, 1850, 1870, 1880, 1900, 1910, 1930, 1940, 1950, 1960, 1970, 1980, 1990l, 2000, 2010, and today. What conclusions can you draw from this data?

3. Refer to the Economic Timetable. What was the federal debt in 1800, 1810, 1820, 1830, and 1835. What conclusion might you draw about the federal government's efforts to pay off the federal debt at that time?

4. According to the Economic Timetable, when did the federal government give up any attempt to pay off the federal debt?

For Further Reading

5. HOW MUCH IS A MILLION by David M. Schwartz (for ages 6-10), published by HarperCollins.

6. IF YOU MADE A MILLION by David M. Schwartz (for ages 6-10), published by HarperCollins.

The Roaring '90s

For Research and Discussion

1. After reading "The Roaring '90s" and Uncle Eric's explanation for the stock market boom of the 1990s and the stock market crash of 2008, listen to politicians and read mainstream news articles, and then compare their explanations for the stock market crash of 2008 to Uncle Eric's explanation.

Chapter 12: What's So Bad About the Federal Debt?

Short Answer/Fill-in/True or False

1. What is a job?

2. From where does the money for tools come?

Discussion/Essay/Assignment

3. Complete the "Interesting Exercise" that directly follows the chapter *What's So Bad About the Federal Debt?* in WHATEVER HAPPENED TO PENNY CANDY?

For Further Reading

4. Read *The Nature of Work* (page 76) by Robert LeFevre, for ages 12 and up, and *The Tale of the Little Red Hen* (page 81) by W.A. Paton, for ages 9 and up.

One Reason Governments Spend So Much

Short Answer/Fill-in/True or False

1. List the three stages in which industries develop.

   1.

   2.

   3.

2. Can you list any other examples, besides the airline industry, in which government moved forward, once science and engineering feasibility had been proven, even though the costs were greater than the benefits?

The Nature of Work
by Robert LeFevre
(for parents, teachers, and others ages 12 and up)

Work means the application of one's energies toward the accomplishment of a given task. In a sense, the application of one's energies, even when there is no task to be performed, is a kind of work. We could say, for example, that a man who is lolling under a shade tree is "employed" in day-dreaming. Normally, we don't refer to actions of this kind as work. When we talk about work, we usually mean that a goal has been established and means are being employed toward the attainment of that goal. However, a man who is engaged in a sport activity is "working" at it. A man who has become destructive and is trying to rob a bank or a filling station is "working." In common usage, we reserve the word *work* for our constructive goals. So, if the goal is not constructive, we say that the man is playing or loafing. And if he is robbing a bank, we say that he is engaged in robbery and we don't dignify that action by calling it work.

Begin thinking of your child as a worker. Certainly, he is going to play and day-dream and waste a good deal of time. This is only to be expected of any individual who doesn't really know what to do and hence doesn't know which means to adopt in order to employ his energies. The more quickly your child accepts certain goals as his own, the more quickly you can help him learn the proper means for the accomplishment of those goals. Work, as used here, will be limited to goal-oriented procedures of a constructive nature.

Interestingly enough, the child may resist the idea of working at the outset. This is usually because he doesn't understand what he is to do or why he is to do it. Children really enjoy being busy. And it is no hardship for them to be busy constructively. Actually, they are going to be "working" one way or another, in that they will certainly be engaged in expending their energies. The child who understands reality and how he fits into it will have an enormous advantage over the child who doesn't. The former will very soon find things that he wants to do. Because he is motivated by what he wants to do, he will be eager to discover the ways and means to proceed in the direction he wishes to go.

The Joy of Working

How important is it that a person work? Most people stress economic necessity, indicating that if you don't work, you won't earn the money by means of which you can be self-supporting. This is true enough, but it is only part of the story. Factually, you and your child are going to be engaged in expending your energies. And the happiest and most successful people are those who work and work hard.

To begin with, the work of your child is going to be concentrated to a large degree in various learning processes. Make no mistake about it, that, too, is work. It takes discipline, concentration, self-control, and commitment to be either a good student or a good teacher. But the whole purpose of education is to assist the individual in putting his knowledge to work. To know something for the sake of knowing it may be fine. But to know something that can be used constructively is what we all desire.

Viewing humanity as a whole gives us another insight into the business of work. All men are consumers and their wants and desires are insatiable. We all want more and more things to consume. There is no mystery about it. If those things are going to exist, they will have to be produced.

Somebody is going to have to do the work that makes production possible. Man, by his nature, is a consumer. Educated, mature man is also a producer. We begin life as consumers and we will continue to consume until we die. Production is a learned skill. We don't come into the world prepared to work and to produce and distribute and serve. Children are little, animated appetites and they demand goods and services incessantly.

Look at it this way. An individual will consume during his entire life. But how much of his life will be spent in production? Usually, only the middle portion. When a man is yet a child, he does not produce, as a rule. And when he becomes truly elderly or possibly when he becomes ill or decrepit, he will not be able to produce. So the work span of man is much shorter than his consumption span. What does that mean?

It means that for human life as we know it to continue to exist, and hopefully to be a better life with more opportunities for joy and fulfillment, those of us who are engaged in producing are going to have to produce a great deal. We are going to have to produce enough in our productive years to bridge the much longer time in which we won't be producing.

The Importance of Saving

Human survival is based upon the ability to create surpluses. If we consumed today everything we produced today, we would begin each day in a situation of unbearable want, deprivation, and starvation. Properly, the parents are productive enough so that while they are raising their children they are producing enough to take care of their own wants and also to invest in the wants of the children. Hopefully, when that is accomplished the parents will continue to produce so they can create sufficient surpluses to tide them over their later years when they will not be able to produce enough, or possibly when they cannot produce at all.

There is still another reason why surpluses are important. Every act of production is preceded by an investment of one kind or another. Investments are only possible where surpluses exist. So the more we can produce, the larger our surpluses can become. The larger our surpluses, the more we can invest. The more we can invest, the higher our standard of living and the more constructive our employment. The more constructive our employment, the greater our degree of security and well-being. In short, the more and the better we work, the better for us all.

Interestingly, most of us have been conditioned in our earlier life to look forward to our vacations and our time off from work rather than to our work. This is a complete departure from reality. Vacation times are not necessarily happy times. They may be necessary, just as sleep is necessary. But if a person is correctly educated, he will find work that he will enjoy and he will look forward to it because he can do it well and he gets all kinds of rewards for doing it.

The person who is yearning for vacation and for sleep and for time to loll under a tree as his main interest in life is, to a degree, longing for death. He wants to disconnect from the reality of this world, hoping to find surcease from pain and effort, one way or another. If children are properly educated, they will long to work; they will find great fulfillment in work; and they will work very hard and very long in the attainment of their goals.

The happy man is not he who has nothing to do. Examine the records covering men who retire once they reach the age of sixty-five, either because they are compelled to retire or because they choose to do so. Unless they can find hobbies or some other kind of work that will engross them, their life expectancy is reduced rapidly. Living really means working (i.e., constructively employing one's energies). These are some of the reasons why work is important.

Three Types of Work

Work could be classified in various categories and at several levels. Remember, we are considering only constructive, goal-oriented endeavors. There is *physical work*. This is the employment of our energies, in doing simple tasks where our muscles and bones are employed directly. There is always some measure of skill entailed in any kind of work, even very simple work. A man who digs a ditch, runs a hand lawn-mower, or loads a freight car is using some skills, but the principal demand on him is in the expenditure of his own physical energy.

The next classification would be called *skilled labor*. The skilled worker has learned to deal with machines or mechanisms or power or electronic tools which, in themselves, do most of the work. A typist is a skilled worker. So is a man who drives a tractor, a truck, or a bulldozer, or who operates a linotype machine, a lathe, a drill press, or an electronic calculator. Most of the actual work in such cases is done by the machine. However, very skillful management of those machines is required to keep them doing their best. A skilled worker can work just as hard as a physical worker. But he uses a relatively smaller amount of his own physical energy, concentrating usually on how he moves his fingers, or possibly his arms and legs. Frequently, the skilled worker can sit down as he works, although that is not always possible, depending on the tool he uses.

Then there is the *mental worker*. He employs his brains in the accomplishment of some objective. Mental workers would include both teachers and students, as well as lawyers, writers, analysts, researchers, and inventors. Almost always there is a certain amount of skilled labor that accompanies mental labor. The teacher must study, and that means getting books and turning pages, and taking trips to see things and possibly experimenting with various tools and substances. And then the teacher must communicate. An architect is a

mental worker, but he also employs the tools of the artist in his craftsmanship. The lawyer must be able to prepare a brief and to argue the case of his client. A writer must not only think what he wants to say, he must do the skillful work of selecting the right words and putting them down on paper. You can think of scores of examples in each of these three categories.

Because mental work is the most difficult, and also the least visible, we often feel that mental workers are somehow superior. This is probably as it should be. To become a competent user of the mind takes some extraordinary skills. Further, in this world we tend to reward mental workers at a rather high rate of pay. So there is a kind of prestige that attaches to mental work, including the advantage of more dollars.

However, this does not mean that there is anything wrong or demeaning about other kinds of work. All kinds of jobs need doing. Housewives do a lot of physical work requiring only modest skills. Also, they do other kinds of work requiring a much higher degree of skill, as when they cook and prepare and plan meals. Additionally, when a housewife becomes a teacher, she is really engaged at the mental level. We demand a very great deal from the housewife.

Rare Skills Rewarded

The businessman and the investor also works very hard in a variety of ways. He has certain very rare skills if he is to succeed. And this will require physical, skilled, and mental energy.

Sometimes, in our economy, we pay the very highest wages, not to those with the best mental ability, but to those with very rare skills. Professional athletes draw salaries that are sometimes two and three times more than heads of giant corporations. Yet all they do is carry a ball very well, or possibly they can knock a ball over a fence better than anyone else. Still others perform in the art world or the theater with its many phases.

Men and women who are skillful in the arts can earn fantastic pay. But the demands upon them are sometimes staggering.

In teaching your child about work it is important that you find out where his motivations and his abilities take him. Naturally, you will want him to advance as far as he can toward his chosen goals. And it might be well to realize that the higher the goal (higher in the senses of the limited numbers of persons able to perform), the more different types of knowledge and skill that will be demanded.

Many parents refrain from giving their children physical chores around the house, feeling that such chores are beneath the child, since he has rather conspicuous talents of a more advanced nature. This may actually stunt the child's development. Few people work any harder physically than a ballet dancer, an opera singer, a housewife, or even a good writer. It takes discipline and untold hours of dedicated practice and commitment to become competent in these fields. They can begin learning muscular coordination, which is always important, by running errands, dusting, sweeping, mowing grass, and carrying packages. If the proper attitude is developed toward work, you will usually find little difficulty in getting your child to do chores around the house.

Perhaps the child feels that his parents are imposing upon him and taking away his freedom when he is asked to help. But this is probably because he wasn't asked in the right way.

A Goal to Achieve

Your child needs to be goal oriented. He will have greater happiness and greater self-assurance if he is active in moving toward something he wishes to accomplish. Activity for your child is not exclusively physical. If the mind of the child is active, and especially when the mind and the body can be active in harmony aimed at an accomplishment, the tendency to feel imposed upon will be reduced or will disappear.

Parents must take care that they don't harm the child by keeping the chores away from him. Also, they should not impose. The important item to bear in mind isn't the amount of work the child does, but his motivation in connection with the work. Curiously the child who busies himself with chores is usually the child who gets more done in other areas, too. Busy people get more done of their own choosing than people who loaf. When the child gets into the habit of loafing, he not only will not help but he probably won't even help himself.

The child who is thought of as important, not only in what he does but in what he thinks, is usually well adjusted. He feels that he is part of the team, that the team wouldn't function quite as well without him. He will begin taking pride in the things he does and he will find ample time to pursue his own development as he begins setting major goals for himself.

Of overarching importance is the child's mental and moral outlook. If the child becomes convinced, as a result of his early training, that one of the most important things he can do is to become self-supporting so that he "hurts no man," including his parents, and if, at the same time, his parents trust him and consult him and listen seriously and even gravely to his observations, even though he will reveal his lack of experience, that child will probably be happy. And the groundwork will have been laid to make him successful.

The Appropriate Attitude

In our present situation, work is looked down upon as an evil. It is viewed, of course, as necessary. But it is a necessary evil. If you will go to work to eliminate this kind of thinking in your home and certainly with your child, the rewards to you will be substantial.

No child will be happy if his parent sneers at him as a result of the work he does. Sometimes parents unintentionally begin to nag their children, feeling that their offspring could do so much more and so much better than they are doing. So they keep prodding with little remarks dropped from time to time to indicate a lack of satisfaction in their children's behavior. Usually, this will not have the result the parents desire.

When a child embarks upon a task and doesn't do a good job, the parent should exhibit a good sense of proportion and humor. And he should focus his attention upon the job, not upon the child, if the work is done badly. Instead of saying: "Mary, *you* can do better than that," it would be better to say: "Mary, I think it is possible for *that job* to be done better." Then, don't scold or find fault with the person. Stick with the reality of the job requirements.

Possibly the reason the task was poorly performed was that Mary didn't quite understand how to do it. Perhaps you have already shown her. But remember, her mind may have been engaged elsewhere and she only partially understood. You must exhibit the same degree of patience on such an occasion as you would want from your employer if you turned in a poor performance Be sure that your child understands the nature of the task. Equally important, be sure the child knows *why* the task must be performed. Although it may seem obvious to you, remember, your child knows a great deal less about reality than you do. He may not have understood why the floors have to be kept clean. Be sure the child learns as much about it as you know. Also, be careful not to insist on the performance of chores simply on the basis of your authority. "Mary, I told you to do the dishes."

"Why, Mommy?"

"Because I told you to."

This is no answer insofar as the child's curiosity is concerned. Her busy mind, in this case, may be considering the advisability of having each person clean up his own dishes. Or possibly the desirability of never cleaning any of them might occur. What harm would it be if everyone just got his own dirty dishes back again?

Don't laugh at the child, laugh at the task. This makes the burden lighter. Explain the consequences of not doing the dishes.

If the child seems willful, sometimes an example can be provided. Get all the dishes done except Mary's and let her have her own dirty dishes back again, at the next meal.

When Mary begins taking pride in her accomplishments and when she sees that they are important and make her a respected and valued member of the family team, you'll be well on your way toward instilling the value of work.

Reprinted with permission of the Foundation for Economic Education, 30 S. Broadway, Irvington-on-Hudson, New York 10533, web address: http://fee.org

The Tale of the Little Red Hen

W. A. Paton

(for ages 9 and up)

Early one morning the Little Red Hen was out looking for something to eat, and in the course of her search she came upon several plump, fresh kernels of wheat, spilled by somebody in the road. She was just about to swallow them when the thought occurred to her that perhaps she might instead get into the wheat business in a small way by planting the kernels. So she called to some of her farm friends: "Look, I've found some wheat. Who will help me dig up some ground so that we can plant this wheat and raise a crop?"

The "friends" didn't take kindly to the idea. "Not I," quacked the duck. "Not I," honked the goose. "Not I," grunted the pig.

"Well, I will then," said the Little Red Hen. She picked out a nice piece of ground near the fence and worked hard scratching it up into good loose soil. Then she made some holes, well spaced, dropped a kernel in each hole, and filled them carefully with dirt.

The Little Red Hen visited her bit of wheat field every day, pulled out the weeds that came up, used her sprinkling can to water the soil when there wasn't enough rain. Soon the green wheat sprouts broke through the ground and grew into sturdy plants, and finally the stalks and wheat heads appeared and ripened. When the wheat was ready to cut, the Little Red Hen appealed to her "friends" again: "Who will help me cut the wheat and take it to the mill?"

"Not I," said the duck. "Not I," said the goose. "Not I," said the pig.

"Well, I will then," said the Little Red Hen. She cut the wheat stalk by stalk with her shears, bound it into several bundles and carried each bundle on her back over the hill and down by the river to the mill. The miller spread the wheat out on his threshing floor and pounded the heads with his flail until the kernels were all separated from the husks. Then he blew away the straw and chaff and ground the beautiful red wheat into flour. He put the flour in a sack (after taking out his toll for the work he'd done), tied up the sack, and gave it to the Little Red Hen. She carried it on her back all the way home—a long, hard trip. When she had the sack of flour safely in her house, she went out and called to her "friends" once more. "Who will help me make my flour into dough and bake it into bread?"

"Not I," said the duck. "Not I," said the goose. "Not I," said the pig.

"Well, I will then," said the Little Red Hen. She bustled about making the flour into dough, and putting it in her round baking pan. After the dough had risen, she put it in the oven and late in the afternoon she took it out (being careful not to burn herself), and there on the table was a round loaf of the loveliest brown bread anyone ever saw or smelled!

The Little Red Hen then went to the door and—with a bit of a glint in her eye—called out: "Who will help me eat this lovely loaf of bread that I have baked?"

"I will," quacked the duck, very loudly. "I will," promptly honked the goose. "I will," squealed the pig. And all three rushed to the door of the Little Red Hen's house.

But they didn't get any encouragement from that point on. "No," said the Little Red Hen. "I found the wheat; I prepared the soil and planted it; I pulled the weeds and watered the ground when it got too dry; I cut the wheat and carried it all the way to the mill; I carried the flour home myself; I made the flour into dough and baked it. None of you would help until it came to time to eat. And I'm going to eat *my own bread* all by myself." She shut the door with a bang, and sat down to a good meal of hot bread, with plenty of butter on it! And it didn't bother her a bit that she was not sharing the results of her foresight, initiative, and labor with those unwilling to contribute to production but very eager to consume what someone else had produced.

*   *   *

Unfortunately, the fable's ending doesn't square with the facts of life in 1961 America. The duck, the goose, and the pig, constituting a democratic majority, have authorized their income tax collector to take from the very productive little hen up to nine-tenths of the bread she has earned. Added to this ruinous levy there may be a sizable fine to which she is subject for having grown wheat in excess of the quota allowed her under the farm price-support program. Far from enjoying the whole loaf she produced by her own efforts, she'll be lucky in 1961 if her "needy" neighbors leave her as much as a crumb.

Reprinted with permission of the Foundation for Economic Education, 30 S. Broadway, Irvington-on-Hudson, New York 10533, web address: http://fee.org

Chapter 13: Summary

Short Answer/Fill-in/True or False

1.   True or False: Inflation is an increase in the amount of money.

2.   When the amount of money goes up, the value of the money goes _____.

3.   True or False: Inflation is rising prices.

4.   True or False: Inflation causes business people to make mistakes.

5.   True or False: Inflation causes recessions and depressions.

6.   Name one reason the Dark Ages lasted so long.

Discussion/Essay/Assignment

7.   Visit *The Daily Bell* online at www.thedailybell.com. This site (out of Switzerland) is recommended for its free market analysis of economic issues. *The Daily Bell* reprints articles from around the world followed by free-market analysis. [NOTE: Since topics other than economics can be discussed, parental guidance is suggested.] *The Daily Bell* also has guest interviews. To stay current with economic events as they unfold, and to read a point of view that is not usually given through mainstream media, visit *The Daily Bell*. As an exercise, select an economic topic that network television is reporting on, then see if that same topic has been addressed at *The Daily Bell*. If so, compare and contrast the points of view.

Thought Questions

Before you began to read WHATEVER HAPPENED TO PENNY CANDY? you were asked to answer the following questions:

8.   Write an essay explaining what you currently know about economics. Also answer the following question: How important is economics in a person's everyday life?

9.   What do you think is the root cause of America's economic problems?

10. In the course of one day, how often do you discuss economics or seek out news regarding the economy?

Review your answers to the above three questions. Now that you have finished reading WHATEVER HAPPENED TOPENNY CANDY? would you change your answers in any way? Explain.

11.   Now that you have read WHATEVER HAPPENED TO PENNY CANDY? and completed this study guide, write an essay titled "Why It's Important to Study Economics." Compare this essay with the one you wrote earlier, if you completed the earlier assignment.

For Further Reading and Research (Discuss findings or write an essay):

12.   Secure copies of THE MAINSPRING OF HUMAN PROGRESS by Henry Grady Weaver, published by the Foundation for Economic Education (for ages 14 and up), *or* THE DISCOVERY OF FREEDOM by Rose Wilder Lane, published by Fox and Wilkes (for ages 14 and up, but a more difficult read than THE MAINSPRING OF HUMAN PROGRESS). As you read one of these books, determine which civilizations lasted the longest. When did they begin and when did they end? According to THE MAINSPRING OF HUMAN PROGRESS or THE DISCOVERY OF FREEDOM, which civilizations were the most prosperous and which had the most liberty? What conclusions, if any, can you draw?

On-going Activity

13.   Keep a copy of the Economic Timetable conveniently at your study and reading areas. Whenever you study history or read historical fiction or nonfiction, refer to the economic timetable to determine the economic climate in which the story or event occurs. Most economic history is not included in books. This will help you fill the void.

For Further Reading

14.   Watch the PBS program *Connections* or read the book by the same title written by James Burke and published by Simon and Schuster, ISBN 0-316-11672-6.

15.   Read THE ECONOMIST magazine, which Richard J. Maybury (Uncle Eric) says is the best single source of news and analysis of the world economy. Web address: www.economist. com

What Happened in 2008?

Short Answer/Fill-in/True or False

1.   True or False: Much of the new money created to fund the war following September 11 flowed into real estate.

For Research

2.   After the real estate bubble burst in 2008, when did real estate recover?

The Unknown Shakeout

Short Answer/Fill-in/True or False

1. When Tokyo surrendered in World War II, military production and expenditures ended swiftly. Why were the corrections in the marketplace following the end of World War II less problematic than efforts to correct the 2008 recession?

Chapter 14: Where Do We Go From Here?

Short Answer/Fill-in/True or False

1. True or False: There were more unemployed people in 1940 than in 1931.

Discussion/Essay/Assignment

2. In this chapter it is observed that "a lot of people like to blame their enemies for the inflation and recessions." Note how often an individual, a company, or a politician blames someone else for the current state of the economy.

3. Contact the Foundation for Economic Education, Irvington-on-Hudson, NY 10533. Ask them about the resources they have available to learn about economics. You can also visit their web site at www.fee.org

Chapter 15: Natural Law and Economic Prosperity

Short Answer/Fill-in/True or False

1. Economics and law are both very important to your _____ and _____.

2. A country's economic prosperity, or lack of it, is directly related to its _____.

3. What is the premise of Natural Law?

4. Under Natural Law, who grants an individual's rights to life, freedom and property?

5. List the two fundamental laws identified by Richard J. Maybury (Uncle Eric):
    1)
    2)

6.   What happens when everyone, including government, obeys the two fundamental laws?

7.   What is the premise of Civil Law or Roman Law?

8.   Socialist economics has been rejected, but what kind of law remains entrenched and continues to grow everywhere?

9.   Is financial risk directly related to a country's legal system? Explain.

10.   Of those countries listed on page 107 of WHATEVER HAPPENED TO PENNY CANDY?, what type of legal system does each have? (Refer to pages 109-121 of WHATEVER HAPPENED TO PENNY CANDY?). Which of these countries pose the most risk to an investor, and why?

For Further Reading

11.   Read Richard J. Maybury's books (published by Bluestocking Press): 1) WHATEVER HAPPENED TO JUSTICE? and 2) ANCIENT ROME: HOW IT AFFECTS YOU TODAY. These two books provide the background of America's Natural Law heritage and an example of what happens to a society that ignores Natural Law/Higher Law and replaces it with political law.

Nations and Legal Systems

Discussion/Essay/Assignment

1.   How many nations have an index of economic freedom that is greater than 80? On what system of law are each of those countries based? Compare these countries scores to their current scores. Current scores can be found online (conduct an internet search for "Index of Economic Freedom" web page). Has the score and ranking of the United States changed? If so, discuss how it has changed.

2.   How many nations have an index of economic freedom that is less than 30? On what system of law are each of those countries based?

For Research

3.   Conduct in internet search for "Index of Economic Freedom". Compare the freedom scores of the countries listed on pages 109-121 of WHATEVER HAPPENED TO PENNY CANDY? to the current scores listed on the "Index of Economic Freedom" web page. If you are not able to research the entire list, at least research the top and bottom ten countries listed on page 107 to see what their current scores and rankings are.

Projects

The purpose of the following two activities is to show students how economic forces directly affect their daily lives. Students may choose between the two projects, or both may be assigned.

A Personalized Consumer Price Index

Construct a consumer price index for your family. Make a list of items the family uses. The items should be a combination of durables, nondurables, and services. Nondurables have life spans of a year or less. Examples are toothpaste, paper goods, cellophane tape, clothing, nails, gasoline and oil, newspapers, magazines, cosmetics, and food. Durables typically have life spans of more than a year; examples are radios, TVs, automobiles, bicycles, food mixers, computers, chairs, tables, beds, curtains, refrigerators. Examples of services are haircuts, lawnmower repairs, manicures, and automobile oil changes (labor only).

An index should contain at least twenty items. The more items, the clearer the picture of price movements and their effects on the family. Each item should be described exactly: The specific brand, weight, color, type, etc., and the location where it is purchased.

Visit the same stores weekly and record prices. The prices are added to calculate the cost of a "shopping bag" of goods and services.

Prices at the end of the semester are compared with those at the beginning, and each student compares his/her percentage of change with those of other students. This will demonstrate the uneven effects of inflation.

A Historical Price and Money Supply Survey

Visit libraries or conduct internet searches to compare today's prices and money supply statistics with those experienced by earlier generations. You can study old magazines, newspapers, and catalogs to glean prices from previous decades. As I write this today, an example URL might be Food Timeline [www.foodtimeline.org/foodfaq5.html]. Reference sources such as the STATISTICAL ABSTRACT OF THE U.S. [http://www.census.gov/compendia/statab/] and HISTORICAL STATISTICS OF THE U.S. [http://hsus.cambridge.org/HSUSWeb/HSUSEntryServlet] will also contain price information as well as money supply statistics reaching back to the early 1800s.

Charts comparing yesterday with today can be dramatically revealing. In 1915 a one-pound loaf of bread cost $.07, a quart of milk was $.09 and ten pounds of potatoes were $.15. The money supply in 1915 was $11 billion; in 1988 it was $785 billion. Notice prices have not risen as fast as money supply. The main reason is that advances in knowledge and technology have enabled producers to become more efficient and economical. In other words, a free-market economy gives a downward bias to prices, and this downward bias tends to offset the effects of inflation. [Visit the URL www.computerhistory.org and click on *Timeline of Computer History* for technology advances and pricing information.]

What do you think prices would be today if advances in knowledge and technology had not occurred? Estimate what prices might be if the money supply had not been increased.

Accurate calculations are impossible, but the process of estimation will show how much lives have been changed by inflation. One very quick and dramatic measure is to check the wage and price tables in the back of THE ECONOMIST magazine. By using back issues and deducting consumer price increases from wages over several years, you will see how "real" wages have been in a declining trend since the early 1970s. [Online research can also be done, but always note the source of the site, and remember that all history can be slanted based on the facts historians choose to report.]

Final Exam
Multiple Choice

Multiple Choice

1. Inflation is
    a. Rising prices
    b. An increase in the amount of money
    c. Rising wages
    d. Rising wages and prices
    e. Increasing taxes

2. Deflation is
    a. Falling prices
    b. A decrease in the amount of money
    c. Falling wages
    d. Falling wages and prices
    e. Decreasing taxes

3. Inflation causes
    a. More valuable money
    b. Taxes
    c. War
    d. The wage/price spiral
    e. Stagflation

4. A law of economics is
    a. A ruling passed by congress
    b. A guideline which can be changed
    c. A fact of life which no one can change
    d. Part of the law of gravity
    e. Impossible for you to understand

5. An example of the law of supply & demand is
    a. Rising prices cause rising wages
    b. Rising wages cause rising taxes
    c. The amount of money goes up and the value goes up
    d. The amount of taxes goes up and the value of money goes down
    e. The amount of money goes up and the value goes down

6. Gresham's Law says
    a. Good money drives bad money out of circulation
    b. Bad money drives good money out of circulation

c. Good money circulates rapidly

d. Bad money circulates slowly or not at all

e. Prices will never stop rising

7. During severe inflations, wage/price controls have
   a. Always worked
   b. Usually worked
   c. Worked 92% of the time
   d. Worked 43% of the time
   e. Never worked

8. A depression is
   a. A correction period following an inflation
   b. A short recession
   c. A devaluation
   d. Caused by high unemployment
   e. No longer possible

9. A recession is
   a. A long depression
   b. An incomplete depression
   c. Caused by high unemployment
   d. A devaluation
   e. Worse than a depression

10. Money is
    a. The most valuable thing a person can have
    b. The most worthless thing a person can have
    c. The most easily traded thing people have
    d. Always legal tender
    e. The cause of inflation

Final Exam
Short Answer

Answer the following Questions

1. Why are some coins reeded?

2. What is Gresham's Law? Explain.

3. What does tanstaafl mean? Explain.

4. What did the Roman farmers do when wage/price controls were started?

5. Why have wage/price controls never stopped inflation?

6. What does legal tender mean?

7. What is the difference between recession and depression?

8. What is the business cycle?

9. What is the difference between inflation and deflation?

10. Give five (5) examples of black market activities.

    a.

    b.

    c.

    d.

    e.

11. What does money demand mean?

12. What is velocity?

13. What are the three stages of inflation?

Final Exam
Essay

Select one question from the six listed below and write an essay. Support your position.

1.　Why do you think so few people understand inflation and recession?

2.　Contrary to what some people believe, war is very bad for the economy. Wars almost always bring inflation, and when they do, they are followed by recession or depression. For instance, the Civil War brought runaway inflation to both the North and South, and it was followed by a bad depression. Why do you think wars bring such troubles?

3.　Why do you think history, especially economic history, tends to keep repeating itself?

4.　If you were given enough power, how would you stop the business cycle?

5.　Why do you think counterfeiting is illegal?

6.　Do you agree that money mirrors civilization? Why?

For Further Reading

Contact your favorite book supplier or the publisher to order the following in print titles. Books that are out of print sometimes come back into print, and books that are in print, sometimes go out of print. For books that are no longer in print, contact your librarian or used book supplier.

AMERICA'S GREAT DEPRESSION by Murray Rothbard. Available through Mises.org. Ages 15 and up.

AS RIGHT AS RIGHT CAN BE by Anne Rose, published by Dial Books. Story of how Ron Ronson comes to live way beyond his means, goes into debt, and the repercussions that follow when creditors begin to demand payment. He simplifies his life, recognizing the difference between needs and wants, and regains economic control. Out of print. Check your library. Ages 5 to 8.

ALL THE MONEY IN THE WORLD by Bill Brittain, published by Harper Collins. After catching a leprechaun, young Quentin Stowe gets his wish for all the money in the world — and ends up in big trouble as he, and the rest of the world, begin to experience the repercussions of such ownership. Out of print. Ages 9 to 13.

ARTHUR'S FUNNY MONEY — an I Can Read® book by Lillian Hoban, published by Harper Collins. A good first book for budding entrepreneurs. Arthur and Violet decide to start a bike washing business. Arthur uses his start-up capital to buy supplies, sees the necessity for expanding his services to other items, incurs costs from spoilage of products, keeps his accounts, and learns about "misleading" advertising and unplanned price increases. Ages 5 to 8.

ARTHUR'S PET BUSINESS by Marc Brown, published by Little Brown. Arthur wants a puppy, but first he must prove to his parents that he is responsible enough to take care of a puppy. He decides to prove his responsibility by starting a pet-sitting business. Good story for young readers about entrepreneurship and responsibility. Ages 4 to 9.

A BARGAIN FOR FRANCES — an I Can Read® book by Russell Hoban, published by Harper Collins. Thelma tricks Frances into buying her old tea set and then Thelma uses Frances' money to buy for herself the tea set from the store that Frances really wanted. When Frances discovers the deceit she thinks up a way to get Thelma to trade back. A good introduction to the concept of trading and also the idea of "let the buyer beware."   Ages 5 to 8.

BASIC ECONOMICS by Clarence Carson, published by American Textbook Committee. Ages 15 and up.

BETTER THAN A LEMONADE STAND by Daryl Bernstein, published by Beyond Words Publishing. About the entrepreneurial ventures of the author when he was 15-years old. Offers advice and business suggestions to other would-be entrepreneurs, as well as a list of possible start-up businesses for young people. Ages 9 and up.

THE BERENSTAIN BEARS AND THE TROUBLE WITH MONEY: When little bears spend every nickel and penny, the trouble with money is—they never have any. Published by Random House. Whenever the bear cubs get money for chores, or as a present, they run to the nearest store and spend it—not very sensibly. They never save! Mama and Papa discuss the benefits—or not—of giving an allowance. A great first-money lesson for kids. Ages 5 to 9.

CAPITALISM AND THE HISTORIANS by F.A. Hayek, editor, published by University of Chicago Press. Explodes the myth of labor exploitation under the free market and shows that the Industrial Revolution was the first step toward liberation of the masses. 188 pages, paper. Ages 15 and up.

CAPITALISM FOR KIDS: Growing Up to Be Your Own Boss by Karl Hess, published by Bluestocking Press, phone: 800-959-8586, web site: www.BluestockingPress.com. Written to help young people decide what kind of work they want to do now and in their future. Capitalism for Kids stresses the values of self-reliance, responsibility and independence. "...definitely the best book I have ever seen directed to children on the theory of how to go into business for yourself. ..... this book is really absorbing reading."   - Mary Pride 247 pgs., paper. Ages 13 and up.

THE CLIPPER SHIP STRATEGY by Richard J. Maybury, published by Bluestocking Press, phone: 800-959-8586, web site: www.BluestockingPress.com. Explains how government's interference in the economy affects business, careers, and investments. Practical nuts-and-bolts strategy for prospering in our turbulent economy. An extensive discussion of the business cycle. This book is the second sequel to *Whatever Happened to Penny Candy?* and should be read after *The Money Mystery.* 269 pgs., paper. Ages 14 and up.

COMMON SENSE BUSINESS FOR KIDS by Kathryn Daniels. A common sense first guide for young entrepreneurs about running a successful business. Published by Bluestocking Press, phone: 800-959-8586, web site: www.BluestockingPress.com   For ages 12 and up.

COMPLETION OF THE PACIFIC RAILROAD— MAY 29, 1869 Harper's Weekly Newspaper. Facsimile reprint of historical newspaper—includes a very interesting article titled "What Fixes the Price of Gold?" discussing the legal tender law of 1862. Ages 12 and up.

CONNECTIONS by James Burke, published by Simon and Schuster. Recommended by Richard J. Maybury as an excellent introduction to economic history. Richard Maybury recommends that you "Notice that the parts of the world that brought forth the most advancement and improvement were those that contained the most liberty." Paper. Ages 14 and up.

A DAY'S WORK by Eve Bunting, published by Houghton Mifflin. Outstanding book! Don't miss this wonderful story about the importance of work ethics. Doing an honest day's work for an honest day's pay. Grandfather has a strong sense of honesty and integrity. When he and his grandson make a mistake by weeding the "plants" and leaving the "weeds," Grandpa makes the job right. American Bookseller "Pick of the Lists." 32 pgs., paper. Ages 5 to 8.

DISCOVERY OF FREEDOM by Rose Wilder Lane (daughter of Laura Ingalls Wilder). Lane was convinced that individual liberty was a prerequisite to economic and human progress. "This is a revolutionary work. It picks up and develops the individualistic aspects of the American political thought of Thomas Paine, Thomas Jefferson, James Madison, George Mason, and others...." (from the introduction). Ages 14 and up.

E-MYTH REVISITED by Michael E. Gerber, published by Harper Paperbacks. Why entrepreneurs fail and what to do about it. Provides key ingredients to help you develop a small business. Recommended by Richard Maybury. Excellent! Ages 14 and up.

ECONOMICS IN ONE LESSON by Henry Hazlitt, book published by Three Rivers Press, paper. Considered a classic on free market economics. Ages 14 and up.

ECONOMICS ON TRIAL: Lies, Myths and Realities by Mark Skousen, published by Irwin Professional Publishing. Fills in the gaps and corrects the errors in most college level economics books. Ages 16 and up.

THE ENTERPRISING AMERICANS: A Business History of the United States by John Chamberlain. Conduct an online book search. Ages 14 and up.

EXTRAORDINARY POPULAR DELUSIONS AND THE MADNESS OF CROWDS by Charles Mackay, published by Dover Value Editions. Originally published in 1841, here is a serious but frequently hilarious study of mass madness, crowd behavior, and human folly. Traces a broad range of scams, manias, and deceptions including Tulipomania (mentioned in Richard J. Maybury's WHATEVER HAPPENED TO PENNY CANDY?). "If you read no more of this book than the first hundred pages—on money mania—it will be worth many times its purchase." —Andrew Tobias. Ages 14 and up.

FIAT MONEY INFLATION IN FRANCE by Andrew D. White, visit Mises.org or conduct an internet search. Explanation of inflation, its causes, its development and consequences, using Revolutionary France as the example. Essential reading according to Richard J. Maybury. Ages 16 and up.

ECONOMICS: A FREE MARKET READER, published by Bluestocking Press, phone: 800-959-8586, web site: www. BluestockingPress.com. Ages 13 and up.

GO-AROUND DOLLAR by Barbara Johnston Adams, published by Simon and Schuster. Explores the life cycle of the dollar bill from the time it leaves the Bureau of Printing and Engraving and goes into circulation, to the time it finally returns to the Federal Reserve Bank to be destroyed. Interweaves a fictionalized story of the travels of a single dollar bill with facts and anecdotes about the history of the dollar, the printing process, and the symbols found on a dollar bill. Ages 6 to 9.

HOW MUCH IS A MILLION by David M. Schwartz, published by HarperCollins. This is a great book that graphically captures just how much a million really is. WHATEVER HAPPENED TO PENNY CANDY? author Richard J. Maybury says, "written and beautifully illustrated for young children but probably revealing to many adults. Helps you grasp the size of a million, billion, and trillion. Makes the enormity of the government's debt more understandable—and frightening." Ages 6 to 9.

HOW WE LIVE by Red G. Clark and Richrd S. Rimanoczy, available through Christianbook.com, published by Christian Liberty Press. This small booklet has been called "the world's best selling economic primer. More than 8,000,000 copies have been distributed in six languages." Its authors, founders of The American Economic Foundation, predicted that the greatest weakness of self-government would be mass ignorance of the economic principles under which every free economy must operate. Status of publisher, unknown. Try a used book store or book search service. Ages 14 and up.

HUMAN ACTION by Ludwig von Mises, published by Liberty Fund, Inc. The bible of Austrian economics. One of the two general texts recommended by the Ludwig von Mises Institute for the study of Austrian Economics. A very deep book and one that should probably be read when an excellent understanding of free market economics has been mastered. Ages 17 and up.

IF AT FIRST.... by Sandra Boynton, published by Little Brown. Out of print. A delightful story of the never-ending efforts of a small mouse to move an elephant up a hill. Much the same spirit as THE LITTLE ENGINE THAT COULD. Check with your library. Ages 5 to 8.

IF YOU MADE A MILLION by David M. Schwartz, published by HarperCollins. Ages 6 to 9.

THE INCREDIBLE BREAD MACHINE by Susan Love Brown and others, published by Fox & Wilkes. A group of young people assemble information that counters the belief that government intervention is good and private enterprise evil. Ages 13 and up.

THE LITTLE ENGINE THAT COULD by Watty Piper, published by Grosset & Dunlop. A classic about a hard-working train engine that made it up the mountain, through hard work, perseverance, and a belief in himself. Ages 5 to 9.

THE MAINSPRING OF HUMAN PROGRESS by Henry Grady Weaver, by the Foundation for Economic Education (see www.archive.org). According to the Foundation for Economic Education, Mainspring tops all books as a starter for any aspiring student of liberty and economics. It is an exciting streamlined history with maximum information in minimum reading time. Excellent overview of world history. MAINSPRING is an adaptation of Rose Wilder Lane's DISCOVERY OF FREEDOM. Ages 14 and up.

THE MONEY MYSTERY: The Hidden Force Affecting Your Career, Business, and Investments by Richard J. Maybury, published by Bluestocking Press, phone 800-959-8586, web site: www.BluestockingPress.com. Some economists refer to this force as velocity, others to the demand for money. Whichever term is used, it is one of the least understood forces affecting your life. Knowing about velocity and the demand for money not only gives you an understanding of history that few others have, it prepares you to understand and avoid pitfalls in your career, business, and investments. THE MONEY MYSTERY is the first sequel to WHATEVER HAPPENED TO PENNY CANDY? and provides essential background for getting the most from THE CLIPPER SHIP STRATEGY. Ages 14 and up.

MYTH OF THE ROBBER BARONS: A New Look at the Rise of Big Business in America by Burton Folsom, published by Young America's Foundation. Highly recommended by Richard J. Maybury. Folsom draws a distinction between true entrepreneurs who operated via the free market and monopolists who depended primarily on state favors. Ages 14 and up.

PLANNED CHAOS by Ludwig von Mises. URL: mises.org. An essay on the destruction of individual liberty by totalitarian ideologies. Compares socialism, fascism, communism, and welfare statism. Ages 16 and up.

ROAD TO SERFDOM by F.A. Hayek, published by University of Chicago Press. Warnings of the dangers of government intervention. Recommended by Richard J. Maybury. Ages 15 and up.

ROUND AND ROUND THE MONEY GOES by Melvin and Gilda Berger, published by Ideals Childrens Books. Explains the development of money, from its orgins in the barter system to its modern usage as cash, checks and credit cards. First few pages show a good example of velocity as explained in WHATEVER HAPPENED TO PENNY CANDY? by Richard Maybury. Ages 7 to 10.

THROTTLING THE RAILROADS by Clarence Carson. Article available through thefreemanonline.org. How government intervention had a disastrous impact on the railroads. Ages 14 and up.

A TIME FOR TRUTH by William E. Simon, published by Berkeley Publishing. Out of print. Simon explains the danger of government intervention in the economy from first-hand experience as Secretary of the Treasury. Ages 14 and up

UMP'S FWAT available to read at www.powellcenter.org/publications.asp. A clever and entertaining way of showing how a business evolves and how its profits create jobs and useful products. Ages 10 and up.

UNCLE ERIC TALKS ABOUT PERSONAL, CAREER, AND FINANCIAL SECURITY by Richard J. Maybury, published by Bluestocking Press, phone 800-959-8586, web site: www.BluestockingPress.com. Maybury discusses the benefits of educating children for entrepreneurial careers, rather than preparing them to be employees for the other guy. Ages 14 and up.

UNCLE ERIC'S MODEL OF HOW THE WORLD WORKS by Richard J. Maybury, published by Bluestocking Press, phone 800-959-8586, web site: www.BluestockingPress.com. Includes every book in the Uncle Eric series published through 1998: 1) UNCLE ERIC TALKS ABOUT PERSONAL, CAREER AND FINANCIAL SECURITY, 2) WHATEVER HAPPENED TO PENNY CANDY? 3) WHATEVER HAPPENED TO JUSTICE? 4) ARE YOU LIBERAL? CONSERVATIVE? OR CONFUSED? 5) ANCIENT ROME: HOW IT AFFECTS YOU TODAY, 6) EVALUATING BOOKS: WHAT WOULD THOMAS JEFFERSON THINK ABOUT THIS? 7) THE MONEY MYSTERY, 8) THE CLIPPER SHIP STRATEGY, 9) THE THOUSAND YEAR WAR IN THE MIDEAST: HOW IT AFFECTS YOU TODAY, 10) WORLD WAR I: HOW IT AFFECTS YOU TODAY, and 11) WORLD WAR II: HOW IT AFFECTS YOU TODAY. Ages 13 and up for WHATEVER HAPPENED TO PENNY CANDY? and Ages 13-14 and up for all other titles in the Uncle Eric series.

THE WAY TO WEALTH by Benjamin Franklin, multiple editions available. First printed in 1758, this book is one of the most important money books ever published, with basic and sound advice such as "Lost time is never found" and "The sleeping fox catches no poultry." Ages 12 and up.

WHAT HAS GOVERNMENT DONE TO OUR MONEY? by Murray Rothbard, published by the Ludwig von Mises Institute (mises.org). Explains the subject of money in clear and simple language. Essential reading according to Richard Maybury. Ages 14 and up.

WHATEVER HAPPENED TO JUSTICE? by Richard J. Maybury, published by Bluestocking Press, phone 800-959-8586, web site: www.BluestockingPress.com. Explains how the economy is affected when the legal system is based on made-up law rather than higher law. Ages 14 and up.

YOUNG ARTIST by Thomas Locker published by Penguin. Adrian is apprenticed to a master artist. He loves to paint landscapes, and paints what he sees. He faces an issue of compromise when he is ordered by the King to paint the royal court. Each member instructs Adrian to paint him/her as they prefer the world to see them, not as they are. How Adrian handles this dilemma is the heart of the story. What a treat! A book that accomplishes so much—beautiful art, a look at apprenticeship, a look at the power and fear generated by kings. (Complementary title—Richard Maybury's WHATEVER HAPPENED TO JUSTICE? Chapter 30—*Origins of Government*). Ages 5 to 10. Out of Print.

YOUNG ENTREPRENEUR'S GUIDE TO STARTING AND RUNNING A BUSINESS by Steve Mariotti, published by Random House. Includes stories of successful entrepreneurs; business suggestions; the philosophy behind entrepreneurship; and the basic knowledge needed to run a business successfully. Also covers the nuts and bolts of start-up: costs, financial statements, return on investment, market research, preparing a business plan, financing, negotiating, making sales calls, record keeping, and more. Ages 14 and up.

Films and Documentaries

If the following films are no longer available, you might conduct an internet search for used copies. They are recommended because they contain good economic history.

AMERICA'S CASTLES series. Produced by the History Channel. Highly recommended by Richard Maybury for its economic history.

AUTOMOBILES series. Produced by the History Channel. Highly recommended by Richard Maybury for its economic history.

CADILLAC DESERT, Part One. Good economic and legal history, from PBS Home Video.

THE GREAT SHIPS: The Clippers. Produced by the History Channel.. Highly recommended by Richard Maybury for its economic history. Terrific supplement to Richard Maybury's THE CLIPPER SHIP STRATEGY.

GREED by John Stossell. Dispells much of the myth about the greedy robber baron capitalist and explains how capitalism works through a system of voluntary exchange. (Conduct an internet search for availability.)

TRAINS UNLIMITED, aired on the History Channel. The story of the Atchison, Topeka, and Santa Fe Railroad, the Harvey Hotels, and the employment of the Harvey girls. Highly recommended by Richard J. Maybury. Good economic history showing how industries develop and how industries affect the development of towns and cities.

Reference Sources

America's Future
7800 Bonhomme
St. Louis, MO 63105
Ph: 314-725-6003
http://www.americasfuture.net/
Dedicated to the preservation of America's free enterprise system and constitutional form of government.

Bluestocking Press
Ph: 800-959-8586
Publisher of the Uncle Eric books by Richard J. Maybury.
Catalog targets business, economics, entrepreneurship, and law
http://www.BluestockingPress.com/

Cato Institute
1000 Massachusetts Ave. NW
Washington DC 20001
Ph: 202-842-0200
Free market think tank.
http://www.cato.org/

The Daily Bell
http://www.thedailybell.com/
Appenzell, Switzerland
"A Daily Compendium of Free-Market Thinking"
Delivers free-market analysis of mainstream news articles.

Foundation for Economic Education
30 South Broadway
Irvington-on-Hudson, NY 10533
Ph: 800-960-4FEE or 914-591-7230
http://www.fee.org/
Information source on free market economics.

Free Enterprise Institute
9525 Katy Fwy Suite 303
Houston, TX 77024
Ph: 713-984-1343; 800-884-2189
http://www.americanidea.org/
Educates teachers in the principles of the American Republic.

Laissez Faire Books
835 W. Warner Rd #101-617
Gilbert, AZ 85233
Ph: Book Orders (toll free): 866 686-7210; office 707 746-8796
http://www.lfb.org
Included here as a source for free market economics titles (both books and DVDs).

LibertyTree Network
100 Swan Way
Oakland, CA 94621
Ph: 800-927-8733 or 510-568-6040
http://www.independent.org/
Online archives and student programs.
http://www.liberty-tree.org
Source for books, and other items related to personal and economic freedom, American history, politics, and more.

Ludwig von Mises Institute
518 West Magnolia Ave.
Auburn, AL 36832-4528
Ph: 334-321-2100
http://mises.org/
Consider themselves to be the world center of the Austrian School of economics. You can sign up for daily emails. They have a bookstore, and also offer free books in their literature section.

National Schools Committee for Economic Education
250 East 73rd Street, Suite 12G
New York, New York 10021-8641
Ph: 212-535-9534
http://www.nscee.org/
Free enterprise lessons for young people.

Mark Skousen
c/o Eagle Publishing Inc.
One Massachusetts Ave. NW
Washington, DC 20001
1-800-211-7661
http://www.mskousen.com/

Web Sites of Interest
(also refer to those websites listed in Reference Sources)

NOTE: When statistics are reported, always consider the source of those statistics. Remind yourself that data can be factual but selected data can distort conclusions. Be certain you trust the source of your data and always ask yourself if the researcher whose work you are studying is astute enough to question the reliability of his/her sources, whether private or government.

Charts: http://www.economagic.com/em-cgi/charter.exe/fedstl/fygfd

CIA Country Factbook: https://www.cia.gov/library/publications/the-world-factbook/index.html

The Economist: www.economist.com

Federal Reserve Bank of St. Louis: http://research.stlouisfed.org/fred2/

Freedom House: www.freedomhouse.org

The Heritage Foundation: http://www.heritage.org/

Institute for Humane Studies: http://www.theihs.org/

Mackinac Center for Public Policy: http://www.mackinac.org/

Measuring Worth: http://measuringworth.com

Statistical Abstract of the U.S.: http://www.census.gov/compendia/statab/

U.S. National Debt Clock web site:
     http://www.brillig.com/debt_clock/
     http://usdebtclock.org
     http://www.defeatthedebt.com/

Stamp's Law

"The government are very keen on amassing statistics. They collect them, add them, raise them to the nth power, take the cube root and prepare wonderful diagrams. But you must never forget that every one of these figures comes in the first instance from the chowty dar (village watchman), who just puts down what he .... pleases." (Stamp recounting a story from Harold Cox who quotes an anonymous English judge).

— Josiah Stamp (1929)
Some Economic Factors in Modern Life. P. S. King & Son. pp. 258–259

Answers to Study Guide Questions

Author's Disclosure and Point of View

Short Answer/Fill-In/True or False

1. Juris Naturalism is the belief in a Natural Law that is higher than any government's law.

Discussion/Essay/Assignment

2. Answers will vary, but students should note that the bias or philosophical slant of an author, news commentator, or reporter can influence the selection of facts included in a book or report, thereby slanting the history, or other subject areas.

3-6. Answers will vary.

Thought Questions

Answers will vary to thought questions 1, 2, and 3. Save the student's responses. The student will be asked to revisit these questions and answers.

For Discussion

Answers will vary. Determine if the student has correctly identified the differences between needs and wants based on the examples supplied.

Preface

1. WHATEVER HAPPENED TO PENNY CANDY? is based on the Austrian and Monetarist schools of economic theory.

2. The origins of the terms for these schools of economic theory are: 1) Austrian because the founders of the Austrian school were from Austria. 2) Monetarist because these economists place great importance on the quantity of money circulating in the economy.

3. The individuals who are representative of these schools of economics include:
   Alan Greenspan, Chairman of the Federal Reserve System, Austrian
   Friedrich A. Hayek, nobel prize winner, 1974, Austrian
   James M. Buchanan, nobel prize winner, 1986, Austrian
   Milton Friedman, nobel prize winner, 1976, Monetarist, also known as Chicago School.

Discussion/Essay/Assignment

4. Answers will vary.

A Note About Economics

Short Answer/Fill-in/True or False

1. According to Uncle Eric, this book is based on **Austrian** and **Monetarist** economics because good science and good economics depends upon the ability to **predict**.

Chapter 1: Money: Coins and Paper

Define

1. Clad (coin): A sandwich coin. A coin made of layers of different metals.

2. Fine (silver): Purity of a precious metal. For instance, if a coin is 900 fine gold, then it is 90 percent gold.

3. Base metal: A non-precious metal like copper or nickel.

4. Token: A disk of base metal which can be used as a substitute for a coin.

Short Answer/Fill-In/True or False

5. Coins dated 1965 to the present are not coins—they are tokens. A coin is a disk of precious metal, like gold or silver. If the disk contains no precious metal, it is a token.

Discussion/Essay/Assignment

6. Silver was removed from U.S. dimes and quarters in 1965. All gold backing was removed from the U.S. dollar in 1971.

For Research

7. Chances are you will find no coins dated after 1965. The reason follows: Prior to 1965 coins were not clad, but were made of 900 fine silver. When precious metal coins stopped minting, individuals began to save them, thus removing the pre-1965 coins from circulation; they spent the clad coins.

Chapter 2: Tanstaafl, the Romans and Us

Define

1. Double-digit inflation: Price increases rising at 10 to 99 percent per year due to inflation.

2. Welfare program: A government program for giving away money or goods, usually to poor people.

3. Subsidy: A government program for giving tax money away, usually to rich people or large companies.

4. Law of economics: A fact of life which deals with production and distribution of wealth. You cannot change it, and it applies all over the world.

5. Tanstaafl. (Sounds like tans-t-awful) "There Ain't No Such Thing As A Free Lunch." A popular expression during the Great Depression. Means that almost nothing is free, someone must pay for it. Tanstaafl is a law of economics.

6. Counterfeiting: To make something that is fake or phony, i.e. money.

7. Clipping (coins): Shaving the edges of a coin in order to get some of the precious metal from the coin.

8. Reeding: The notches on the edge of a coin.

9. Debasing: Reducing the value of a coin by reducing the amount of precious metal in it.

10. Gresham's Law: A law of economics; says bad money drives good money out of circulation. People hoard good money and trade with legally overvalued money.

Short Answer/Fill-in/True or False

11. During a double-digit inflation the cost of a paperback book that costs $5.00 this year, would cost $5.50 or more next year.

12. Governments tax to provide the goods and services that governments deem necessary.

13. The Federal government assumed the national debt in 1790 and intended to raise the revenue necessary to pay off the debt through import tariffs and excise taxes.

14. Each person's share of the national debt in 1791 was approximately $18.88. (Divide the national debt of $75.5 million by the U.S. population of 4 million cited in 1790 data).

15. The government today counterfeits by printing paper dollars that are not backed by a gold or silver standard. Other methods included: clipping coins and debasing the money.

16. The Continental dollar became worthless during the Revolutionary War because the government printed too many of them.

17. The Roman government counterfeited by clipping coins, meaning they shaved the edges of the coin, then used the shavings to mint, or make, new debased coins. The government would then have the newly minted coins in addition to the clipped coins.

18. Prior to 1965 base-metal coins, those that did not contain gold or silver, were not reeded. Those included pennies and nickels. They weren't worth much, so reeding was not important. But precious-metal coins that contained gold or silver were reeded and included: dimes, quarters, half dollars, silver dollars, which did contain silver until 1965.

19. Today's reeded coins give the illusion that they are still precious in their own right, even though they aren't.

20. By law, Americans must accept the face value of a coin. If it says fifty cents they must accept the value of fifty cents, even though it does not have fifty cents worth of silver in it.

21. By saving precious metal coins and spending coins that contain no precious metals, people are following Gresham's Law which says bad money drives good money out of circulation. People want to save the good money and get rid of the bad money.

22. In 1878 the Bland-Allison Act mandated the U.S. Treasury purchase $2-$4 million in silver bullion per month, which overvalued silver.

23. Gresham's Law has driven good money out of circulation.

Discussion/Essay/Assignment

24. If a taxpayer refuses to pay taxes, then the taxpayer could go to jail.

25. Some people save precious metals coins to protect themselves and their wealth from the possibility of U.S. currency becoming worthless. Also, if America's current paper money and coinage become worthless, they will have precious metal coins to buy necessary goods and services.

For Research

26-27. Answers will vary.

To View

28-30. Answers will vary.

Chapter 3: Inflation

Define

1. Law of supply and demand: Says that when the supply of something goes up, the price per unit of that thing goes down. When the supply goes down the price goes up.

2. Inflation: An increase in the amount of money. Causes the money to lose value, so prices rise.

Short Answer/Fill-in/True or False

3. Statement "A" is true.

4. Answers will vary. Examples: a) Shortage of gasoline in U.S. in 1974 and 1979 drove the price of gasoline up. b) The glut of houses on the market in 2009 and 2010 in the U.S. drove housing prices down. c) The supply of inexpensive restaurant breakfasts drive the prices down in competing restaurants. d) Sold out concert and theater shows cause scalpers to sell tickets at high prices. e) Toilet paper shortage in the the U.S. in 1973.

For Research

5-9. Answers will vary.

Real Investment Value

A. **1)** 88 **2)** .44 or 44% **3)** .694 or 69.4% **4)** $68,012
    5) $20,000 **6)** $6,600 **7)** $91,400 **8)** $63,432, **9)** -$14,568 (loss)

B. **1)** 42 **2)** .21 or 21% **3)** .826 or 82.6% **4)** $182,753
    5) $32,750 **6)** $7,860 **7)** $213,390 **8)** $176,260, **9)** -$12,240 (loss)

C. **1)** zero **2)** zero **3)** 1.00 or 100% **4)** $125,000
    5) $20,000 **6)** $4,800 **7)** $120,200 **8)** $120,200, **9)** $15,200 (profit)

D. **1)** zero **2)** zero **3)** 1.00 or 100% **4)** $200,000
    5) $100,000 **6)** $5,000 **7)** $195,000 **8)** $195,000, **9)** $95,000 (profit)

E. **1)** 88 **2)** .44 or 44% **3)** .694 or 69.4% **4)** $68,012
    5) $20,000 **6)** $1,000 **7)** $97,000 **8)** $67,318, **9)** -$10,682 (loss)

F. **1)** 88 **2)** .44 or 44% **3)** .694 or 69.4% **4)** $68,012
    5) $20,000 **6)** $10,000 **7)** $88,000 **8)** $61,072, **9)** -$16,928 (loss)

G. **1)** 100 **2)** 0.5 or 50% **3)** .667 or 66.7% **4)** $147,574
    5) $32,750 **6)** $7,860 **7)** $213,390 **8)** $142,331, **9)** -$46,169 (loss)

H. **1)** 200 **2)** 1.00 or 100% **3)** 0.5 or 50% **4)** $110,625
    5) $32,750 **6)** $7,860 **7)** $213,390 **8)** $106,695, **9)** -$81,805 (loss)

Chapter 4: Dollars, Money, and Legal Tender

Define

1.   Dollar: a one-ounce ingot of silver.

2,   Money: The most easily traded thing in a society. Economists call it the most liquid commodity.

3.   Coin: A wafer or disk of precious metal. True coins usually have three markings; weight, fineness, and name of mint.

4.   Hallmark: The mint-mark of a coin. Tells who made the coin. Like a trademark.

5.   Banknote: Today, paper money. Originally, an IOU from a bank, usually for gold or silver.

6.   Legal tender law: A law which provides for the punishment of anyone who refuses to accept the legal tender money.

7.   Fiat money: Legal tender money.

Short Answer/Fill-in/True or False

8.   Good money must be small, easy to move, widely desired, corrosion-proof, scarce, and hard to copy.

9.   Throughout the centuries gold and silver have had the characteristics listed in answer number 8.

10.   Shells, beads, stones, furs, grain, and salt are just some of the items that have been used as money throughout the centuries.

11.   Coins were invented to tell a person the weight or quantity of gold or silver they own.   In this way they would know exactly how much gold or silver to exchange for a product or service.

12.   Dollar comes from the word thaler which was a shortened form of the word Joachimthaler, a one-ounce silver coin minted in a place called Joachimthal in Bohemia during the Middle Ages.

13.   Silver certificates are slips of paper representing one dollar banknotes which could be exchanged for silver if you took them to the U.S. Treasury.

14.   Silver certificates did not have legal tender statements. Instead they said: "This certifies there is on Deposit in the Treasury of the United States of America One Dollar in Silver Payable to the Bearer on Demand."

15.   Federal Reserve Notes have replaced Silver Certificates and are being printed in huge quantities. They are not backed by any precious metals; they are just paper. Because of this, our money is worth less today than when it was made of gold or silver.

16.   The legal tender law gives Federal Reserve Notes their value.

17.   If you refuse to accept Federal Reserve Notes in payment of a debt, the debt is cancelled.

18.   Article 1, Section 10 of the U.S. Constitution says that no State shall "make any Thing but gold and silver Coin a Tender in Payment of Debts."

19.   By 2009, according to the government's own Consumer Price Index, the Federal Reserve dollar had lost 95% of the value it had in 1914.

20. Gold coins stopped circulating in the United States in the 1930s. Silver coins stopped circulating in the United States in the 1960s.

21. By allowing the government to forbid the circulation of gold and silver, and requiring everyone to accept paper money, the value of America's money fell and the price of goods and services rose.

Discussion/Essay/Assignment

22. Answers will vary.

For Further Reading

23. The information that is missing in ROUND AND ROUND THE MONEY GOES: 1) U.S. dollars are no longer backed by precious metals. 2) The legal tender law says if someone refuses to accept a Federal Reserve Note in payment of debt, then the debt is cancelled.

24. In the article ETERNAL LOVE, the words "Eternal Love" might be considered the hallmark. A coin is a wafer or disk of precious metal (in this story, platinum). True coins usually have three markings; weight, fineness, and name of mint. The Trans-World Mining Company manufactured the discs and sold them in various sizes. Although it isn't clear from the story if the discs were consistent in weight and fineness, it can be assumed the value was consistent enough to satisfy the demand for them by the consumer.

Chapter 5: Revolutions, Elections, and Printing Presses

Define

1. Revolution: Overthrowing a government, usually by force.

Short Answer/Fill-in/True or False

2. A dictator does not want to be overthrown through revolution by taxing the people too much. So instead of raising taxes, dictators print more money. They inflate.

3. People want to be reelected in a democracy. If taxes are too high a politician might be voted out of office. Instead of raising taxes, a democratic government is likely to print money.

4. Besides using money to inflate, modern politicians use banks and the Federal Reserve to inflate.

Discussion/Essay/Assignment

5. Answers will vary.

Big Mac Index

Discussion/Essay/Assignment

1. Answers will vary.

Chapter 6: Wages, Prices, Spirals, and Controls

Short Answer/Fill-in/True or False

1. The wage/price spiral is the result of inflation.

2. True. Large increases in the supply of money are always followed by increases in wages and prices.

3. True. Large decreases in the supply of money are always followed by a fall in wages and prices.

4. If the unions do not allow wages to fall, then some of the workers will lose their jobs because employers cannot afford to pay them.

5. True. With a few exceptions, there has never been a case where wages and prices rose rapidly without someone creating a lot of money.

Discussion/Essay/Assignment

6-9. Answers will vary.

For Further Reading

10. Answers will vary.

11. Higher prices drove business to the railroads.

12. Answers will vary.

Chapter 7: Wallpaper, Wheelbarrows, and Recessions

Define

1. Runaway inflation: A hyperinflation. Prices rising rapidly, every few hours.

2. Depression: The correction period following an inflation. Usually includes a lot of business failures and unemployment.

3. Recession: The beginning of a depression that never went all the way.

4. Deflation: A decrease in the amount of money. Usually causes depression and falling prices.

Short Answer/Fill-in/True or False

5. The business cycle is the up, down, up, down activity of the government to inflate, stop inflating, inflate, stop inflating. The business cycle is caused by the amount of money being shifted up and down by the government.

For Research

6. Research exercise.

Chapter 8: Fast Money

Define

1. Velocity: The speed at which money changes hands.

2. Demand for money: The desire to hold money rather than trade it away. High demand for money means money is traded away reluctantly. Low demand for money means money is traded away quickly.

Short Answer/Fill-in/True or False

3. If the demand for money decreased people would want to get rid of their money before it became worth less.

4. True. If money demand falls, money changes hands faster.

5. The term for the speed at which money changes hands is the "velocity of circulation."

6. In order for velocity to fall, the demand for money must **rise.**

7. The three stages of inflation are: Stage one: People save their money, waiting for prices to fall. Newly printed money is saved, it does not enter the market, and prices do not rise very fast. Stage two: People decide to spend the newly created money before prices or products increase more than they already have. People speed up their buying. Demand for dollars falls and velocity increases. Money changes hands faster in Stage two of inflation. Prices start to rise faster than money is printed. Stage three: Money is losing its value. People spend their money on products that they do not think will lose their value. People trust products more than money. In the third stage of inflation, money changes hands very quickly. People don't want the money; they are trying to get rid of it and replace it with something of value. Money demand is falling rapidly and velocity is skyrocketing. In the third stage no one can stop the money from losing its value. Things have gone too far. This is runaway inflation.

8. Runaway inflation ends when people completely reject the money and begin using something new for currency. During American runaway inflations, people have usually switched over to gold or silver.

9. People keep velocity under control. Every time an individual makes a decision about spending or keeping his money, he is making a decision about velocity.

10. Two things can cause people to change their spending habits enough to change velocity: 1) Someone tampers with the supply of money, or 2) the government begins to go out of business.

    Examples of tampering with the supply of money: 1) The United States between 1915 and 1929. The government printed money which led to the Roaring '20s and set the stage for the Great Depression that followed.   2) The United States after 2008, massive stimulus packages and new federal programs.

    An example of government going out of business: 1970s North Vietnam when the government went out of business.

11. Inflations do not have to follow the 1, 2, 3 stages described in "Fast Money". They can go from one to two, then back to one again.

Discussion/Essay/Assignment

12. Answers will vary.

For Further Reading

13. Reading exercise.

14. In ROUND AND ROUND THE MONEY GOES, the dollar has been traded four times in the first three pages; the velocity is four.

15. In THE GO-AROUND DOLLAR, the velocity of the dollar Matt finds is seven.

History Repeats

Discussion/Essay/Assignment

1. During the 1920s, investors spent their money on stocks.

2. During the 1990s, investors spent their money on stocks.

3. When the bubble of the 1990s burst, much of the newly created money was spent on real estate.

Chapter 9: Getting Rich Quick

Define

1. Business cycle: The boom/bust cycle. Prosperity followed by recession followed by prosperity followed by recession, and so forth.

Short Answer/Fill-in/True or False

2. An excellent example of America's boom-and-bust cycle is the 1929 Stock Market Crash.

Chapter 10: The Boom and Bust Cycle

Define

1. Stock: Shares of ownership of a company.

Short Answer/Fill-in/True or False

2. M2 defines money as currency, checking accounts, travelers checks, savings accounts, money market mutual funds, and certain transactions between banks.

3. By subtracting price increases from M2 we get the "real" M2 money supply.

4. When government slows the creation of real M2, a recession hits.

5. When the supply of M2 was slowed in 1987, the supply of money to the stock market dried up.

For Research

6. Answers can be found in the Economic Timetable.

Chapter 11: How Much is a Trillion?

For Research

1. Answers will vary.

2. Answers will vary.

3. The federal government actually tried to pay off the debt at one time.

4. The federal government gave up trying to pay off the federal debt around WWI (1917-1918).

The Roaring '90s

For Research and Discussion

1. Answers will vary.

Chapter 12: What's So Bad About the Federal Debt?

Short Answer/Fill-in/True or False

1. A job is primarily the tools necessary to produce what others want to buy.

2. The money for tools comes from savings in the form of stocks, bonds or bank CDs.

Discussion/Essay/Assignment

3. Answers will vary.

One Reason Governments Spend So Much

Short Answer/Fill-in/True or False

1. Industries develop in the following three stages: 1) scientific feasibility, 2) engineering feasibility, and 3) economic feasibility

2. Answers will vary.

Chapter 13: Summary

Short Answer/Fill-in/True or False

1. True. Inflation is an increase in the amount of money.

2. When the amount of money goes up, the value of the money goes **down.**

3. False. Rising prices are a result of inflation.

4. True. Inflation causes business people to make mistakes.

5. True. Inflation causes recessions and depressions.

6. The Dark Ages lasted so long because the feudal governments were brutal and crooked, and there was no reliable currency, making production and trade difficult.

Discussion/Essay/Assignment

7. Answers will vary.

Thought Questions

8-11. Answers will vary.

For Further Reading and Research

12. Answers will vary.

What Happened in 2008?

Short Answer/Fill-in/True or False

1. True. Much of the new money created to fund the war following September 11 flowed into real estate.

For Research

2. As of the third quarter of 2010, there has been no real estate recovery.

The Unknown Shakeout

Short Answer/Fill-in/True or False

1. The corrections in the marketplace following the end of World War II were less problematic because they were allowed to proceed unhindered. By the 2008 recession, the money supply had been so heavily inflated for so many decades that malinvestment was prolific. And, whereas the post-World War II recession was allowed to proceed unhindered, the federal government in 2008 injected mountains of money into the economy, in addition to numerous new laws and regluations, in an effort to correct the 2008 recession. This type of intervention causes recessions to drag on, and complete corrections do not happen.

Chapter 14: Where Do We Go From Here?

Short Answer/Fill-in/True or False

1. True. There were more unemployed people in 1940 than in 1931.

Discussion/Essay/Assignment

2-3. Results will vary.

Chapter 15: Natural Law and Economic Prosperity

Short Answer/Fill-in/True or False

1. Economics and law are both very important to your **economic prosperity** and **individual liberty**.

2. A country's economic prosperity, or lack of it, is directly related to its **legal system**.

3. The premise of Natural Law is that there is a Higher Law than any government's law, and a judge's job is to discover and apply this Higher Law.

4. Under Natural Law, the "Creator" grants an individual's rights to life, freedom, and property.

5. The two fundamental laws identified by Richard J. Maybury (Uncle Eric) are: 1) Do all you have agreed to do, and 2) Do not encroach on other persons or their property.

6. When everyone, including government, obeys the two fundamental laws, the result is liberty, free markets, and rapid economic growth. Investment and job opportunities abound.

7. The premise of Civil Law or Roman Law is that there is no law higher than the government's law and an individual's rights are granted by the government. A judge's job is to apply the government's law no matter what this law requires, even if the government's law violates the two fundamental laws.

8. Socialist economics has been rejected but socialist law, meaning Roman Law or Civil Law, remains entrenched and continues to grow everywhere.

9. Financial risk is directly related to a country's legal system. If a country's legal system is not based on Natural Law, it is subject to the whims of its government—political law can change at any time and without warning.

10. [Legal systems are listed on pages 109-121 in WHATEVER HAPPENED TO PENNY CANDY?] North Korea poses the most risk. Those countries with legal systems based on political law pose the most risk for an investor. They also have less economic freedom, and the economic freedom they do have can change with political whim.

Worst Scores

Sao Tome and Principe, 43.8.   Mixture of Portuguese civil law and local native customary law.

Libya, 43.5. Mixture of Italian colonial civil law and Islamic law.

Comoros, 43.3. Mixture of French colonial civil law and Islamic law.

Dem. Rep. of Congo, 42.8. Mixture of Belgian colonial civil law and local native customary law.

Venezuela, 39.9. Civil law.

Eritrea, 38.5. Very unsettled. Will probably be some mixture of Italian, British, and Islamic law.

Burma, 37.7. Chaotic, heavily socialistic. Not influenced by Natural Law.

Cuba, 27.9. Mostly socialist civil law, with a smattering of U.S. law. All traces of Natural Law have been erased.

Zimbabwe, 22.7. Mixture of Dutch colonial civil law and English colonial common law.

North Korea, 2.00. Combination of German civil law, Japanese civil law, and socialist civil law. Not influenced by Natural Law.

Best Scores

Hong Kong, 90.0. Until the Chinese takeover on July 1, 1997, it was perhaps the world's best application of Natural Law. After July 1, 1997, it is under the control of China and China is very chaotic, very socialist. China has some local customary law. China is not influenced by Natural Law.

Singapore, 87.1. Based on English colonial common law.

Australia, 82.6. Based on English common law

Ireland, 82.2. Based on English common law and native customary law.

New Zealand, 82.0. Based on English common law.

United States, 80.7. Based on English common law. The original Natural Law premise has been almost totally erased and replaced by civil law. But the Bill of Rights still provides a lot of protection against the government. However, the war that began 9-11 has accelerated the undermining of the Bill of Rights.

Canada, 80.5. Based on English common law, except in Quebec, which is French civil law.

Denmark, 79.6. Civil law, with strong Natural Law influence.

Switzerland, 79.4. Civil law, with heavy Natural Law influence.

United Kingdom, 79.0. English Common Law, heavily influenced by civil law.

Nations and Legal Systems

Discussion/Essay/Assignment

1. Seven nations have an index of economic freedom that is greater than 80: Australia, Canada, Hong Kong, Ireland, Singapore, New Zealand, United States. See "Best Scores" (above) for their system of law.

2. Three nations have an index of economic freedom that is less than 30: Cuba, North Korea, and Zimbabwe. See "Worst Scores" (above) for their system of law?

For Research

3. Answers will vary.

Projects

A Personalized Consumer Price Index: Answers will vary.

A Historical Price and Money Supply Survey: Answers will vary.

Final Exam

Multiple Choice

1. B   6. B

2. B   7. E

3. D   8. A

4. C   9. B

5. E   10. C

Short Answer

1. Some coins are reeded to give them the appearance of gold and silver coins. Reeding is a defense against clipping.

2. Bad money drives good money out of circulation. In other words, if there are two types of money in use and the market values one less than the other but the law fixes them at equal values, people will trade with the artificially high money and save the other.

3. Tanstaafl is a slang expression: There Ain't No Such Thing As A Free Lunch. Nothing of value is free, someone must pay for it.

4. Roman farmers stopped bringing their food to market when wage/price controls were started.

5. Wage/price controls never stopped inflation because they have no effect on the supply of money.

6. Legal tender is money because the government says it is. People who do not treat it as money are punished if they are caught.

7. A recession is an incomplete depression. It usually occurs when an inflation is halted temporarily.

8. The business cycle is the "boom-and-bust" cycle: inflation, recession, inflation, recession, etc.

9. Inflation is an increase in the amount of money. It tends to cause rising prices. Deflation is a decrease in the amount of money. It tends to bring falling prices and recessions or depressions.

10. Examples of black market activities include, but are not limited to: Buying, selling, or producing anything that is illegal. During the 1920s, liquor. Today, marijuana, cocaine, heroin. In some places, handguns. Tax evasion. Before 1776, much American trade in manufactured goods was actually smuggling—the government had forbidden Americans to manufacture their own goods because it wanted them to buy the goods from British manufacturers. Before the Civil War, the "underground railway" that smuggled slaves out of the South was a part of the midnight economy.

11. Money demand refers to a person's desire to hold a type of currency rather than spend it.

12. Velocity is the speed at which money changes hands. It is an indicator of money demand.

13. The three stages of inflation are: Stage one: People save their money, waiting for prices to fall. Newly printed money is saved, it does not enter the market, and prices do not rise very fast. Stage two: People decide to spend the newly created money before prices or products increase more than they already have. People speed up their buying. Demand for dollars falls and velocity increases. Money changes hands faster in Stage two of inflation. Prices start to rise faster than money is printed. Stage three: Money is losing its value. People spend their money on products that they do not think will lose their value. People trust products more than money. In the third stage of inflation, money changes hands very quickly. People don't want the money; they are trying to get rid of it and replace it with something of value. Money demand is falling rapidly and velocity is skyrocketing. In the third stage no one can stop the money from losing its value. Things have gone too far. This is runaway inflation.

Final Exam Essay: Answers will vary.

Economic Timetable

Year	Colonial & U.S. Economic History	Other Historical Events	Movie tie-in	For Further Reading	For Further Study
0310		To halt Rome's ruanaway inflation, emperor Constantine mints gold bezant which becomes most trusted money in history—retains value undebased for 800 years. Bezant is also known as solidus, from which we get our word solid.			
1492		Columbus' voyage to America.			
1607		First permanent English colony in North America is established in Jamestown.			
1610		English colonists experience the "starving time." Colonial population: 210			THE COLONIAL EXPERIENCE by Clarence Carson-the early colonies in Virginia
1620		Pilgrims land at Plymouth and sign *Mayflower Compact.*		Read the *Mayflower Compact*	COLONIAL EXPERIENCE by Clarence Carson-the early colonies in New England
1684		First excise tax on liquor is in effect in Pennsylvania.			
1690		Paper money is issued in Massachusetts. Colonial population: 213,000			
1711		Parliament prohibits Americans from cutting trees in the colonies. All lumber is reserved for use by the Royal Navy.			*The Founding Fathers: Smugglers, Tax Evaders and Traitors?* in EVALUATING BOOKS: WHAT WOULD THOMAS JEFFERSON THINK ABOUT THIS? by Richard Maybury
1750		Reverend Jonathan Mayhew gives sermon "On Unlimited Submission To Rulers," arguing that there is a Higher Law than any government's law. John Adams said this sermon was "read by everybody" and eventually led to the American Revolution.		Read *Jonathan Mayhew's Sermon*	
1764	British Parliament enacts Sugar Act to raise money in the colonies to pay British war debt.				
1765	Stamp Act enacted. Colonial policy of nonimportation of British goods goes into effect. Quartering Act requires colonials to house and feed British troops.	Stamp Act Rebellion.			

Year	Colonial & U.S. Economic History	Other Historical Events	Movie tie-in	For Further Reading	For Further Study
1766	Stamp Act repealed (London merchants cite business failures since Colonials weren't buying their goods).				
1767	Townshend Acts passed (Colonials have to pay import duties on tea, glass, lead, oil, paper, and painter's colors). Nonimportation policy goes into effect once again by the Colonials.				
1770	Townshend Acts repealed. Tax on tea retained. Nonimportation repealed by Colonials.	Boston Massacre. Colonial population: 2.2 million.		THE FIFTH OF MARCH by Ann Rinaldi	
1773		Tea Act leads to Boston Tea Party.	*Johnny Tremain* 1957 Disney film	JOHNNY TREMAIN by Esther Forbes	
1774	Intolerable Acts passed.	Port of Boston closed until payment for tea is made. Colonists must quarter British soldiers. First Continental Congress meets in Philadelphia. Shakers arrive in New York.			
1775		Patrick Henry's speech. Battles of Lexington and Concord. Second Continental Congress meets in Philadelphia. First abolition society established in Philadelphia under Benjamin Franklin and Benjamin Rush.	*1776* based on the Tony award-winning Broadway musical	APRIL MORNING by Howard Fast	
1776		COMMON SENSE by Thomas Paine is published. Congress signs *Declaration of Independence.*		COMMON SENSE by Tom Paine *Declaration of Independence*	
1781	Continental dollar worthless. Depression begins. Congress charters Bank of North America.	American Revolution ends. Articles of Capitulation signed at Yorktown. *Articles of Confederation* established.		*Articles of Confederation*	
1786		Shay's rebellion.		THE WINTER HERO by James L. Collier & Christopher Collier	
1787		*U.S. Constitution* written. Federal government created upon ratification.	*A More Perfect Union* and *Two Good and Noble Men* by National Center for Constitutional Studies	SHH! WE'RE WRITING THE CONSTITUTION by J. Fritz FEDERALIST PAPERS and ANTI-FEDERALIST PAPERS published by Penguin	

Year	U.S. Economic History	Other Historical Events	Movie tie-in	For Further Reading	For Further Study
1789		French Revolution. New French government decides to finance itself with paper money—great French hyperinflation begins.			
1790	Federal government assumes national debt. Revenue is raised by import tariffs and excise taxes.	U.S. population: 4 million			
1791	U.S. federal debt $75.5 million. First internal revenue law passed by Congress. A tax of 20 to 30 cents a gallon is put on alcoholic beverages.	U.S. *Bill of Rights* and *Constitution* finalized.			
1792	Mint established in Philadelphia. Coinage Act specifies U.S. dollar as 416 grains of 892.4 fine silver, or 24.75 grains of 999 fine gold. Official policy "bimetallism." New York Stock Exchange established.	Republican Party, led by Jefferson, (later Democratic-Republican) formed to oppose Federalists. Republicans oppose strong central government.		ARE YOU LIBERAL? CONSERVATIVE? OR CONFUSED? by Richard J. Maybury, published by Bluestocking Press	
1794		Whiskey rebellion squelched (farmers protest excise tax placed on alcoholic beverages in 1791).			
1796		Washington's FAREWELL ADDRESS warns against U.S. political and military involvement in foreign affairs.		WASHINGTON'S FAREWELL ADDRESS published by Applewood	
1800	U.S. federal debt $83 million.	Federal government moves from Philadelphia to Washington D.C. U.S. population: 5.3 million (includes 800,000 slaves).			
1801		Barbary Wars begin.			
1802	Government repeals excise taxes.				
1803		Louisiana Purchase.		Louisiana Purchase	
1807	Congress passes Embargo Act which prohibits U.S. trade with any foreign country.				
1808	First economic calamity of 19th century. "Federal embargo on overseas shipping produced widespread bankruptcies and unemployment," according to the article *How Government Intervention Plagued Our 19th Century Economy*, see page 44 of this book.	Importation of African slaves prohibited by Congress.			*How Government Intervention Plagued Our 19th-Century Economy*, see page 44 of this book

Year	U.S. Economic History	Other Historical Events	Movie tie-in	For Further Reading	For Further Study
1810	U.S. federal debt $53.2 million.	U.S. population: 7.2 million (includes 1.2 million slaves)			
1812		War of 1812. Treaty of Ghent signed December, 1814, ending the war.		AN AMERICAN ARMY OF TWO by Janet Greeson, published by Carolrhoda	
1816	Second Bank of U.S. created.				
1819	Depression begins, lasts till 1823. "Collapse follows credit expansion by the Second Bank of the U.S." according to *How Government Intervention Plagued Our 19th Century Economy,* see page 44 of this book.				Ph.D thesis by Murray Rothbard, *The Panic of 1819.* Query The Ludwig von Mises Institute: http://mises.org/
1820	U.S. federal debt $91 million.	U.S. population: 9.6 million			
1830	U.S. federal debt $48.6 million.	U.S. population: 12.8 million			
1835	U.S. federal debt $38,000. (Yes, believe it or not, they once felt an obligation to pay off the debt. They continued to try to pay off federal debt up until the U.S. got into WWI).				
1837	Depression begins, lasts till 1843 due to Second Bank's rapid expansion of the money supply.				*How Government Intervention Plagued Our 19th-Century Economy,* see page 44 of this book
1840	Congress enacts Independent Treasury Act, which establishes subtreasuries in U.S. cities. Federal funds will be deposited in these new treasuries, payment to be made in coined money.	U.S. population: 17 million			
1846		Irish potato famine. U.S. declares war on Mexico.			
1847		Irish immigration to U.S.: 105,000. Northern whites fear lower wages and poorer working conditions due to Irish immigrants who are willing to work for less. Also fear possibility of freed slaves moving North, another labor source.		DEAR AMERICA: SO FAR FROM HOME — THE DIARY OF MARY DRISCOLL, AN IRISH MILL GIRL, LOWELL, MA 1847, published by Scholastic	
1848	Gold discovered in California. Inflation of U.S. money supply begins.	Revolutions in France, Austria, Italy, Germany, and Poland. Marx & Engle's *Communist Manifesto.*			

Year	U.S. Economic History	Other Historical Events	Movie tie-in	For Further Reading	For Further Study
1850	U.S. federal debt $63.5 million.	Henry Clay opens debate on slavery. THE LAW by Frederic Bastiat is published. U.S. population: 23.1 million (includes approx. 3 million slaves).			THE LAW by Frederic Bastiat WHATEVER HAPPENED TO JUSTICE? by Richard J. Maybury
1851		UNCLE TOM'S CABIN by Harriet Beecher Stowe is published.		Read UNCLE TOM'S CABIN by Harriet Beecher Stowe	
1853	Congress authorizes coinage of $3 dollar gold pieces; reduces amount of silver in all coins except the silver dollar.				
1854	Recession begins.	Chinese immigration: 13,000 for employment on railroad construction.			
1857	Depression begins, resulting from state government intervention in state-chartered banks.				*How Government Intervention Plagued Our 19th-Century Economy*, see page 44 of this book
1860	U.S. federal debt $64.9 million.	Abraham Lincoln elected President.			
1861	Congress enacts income tax to finance Civil War: 3% on incomes over $800. It increases in the following years, supplying one fifth of the federal government revenue by 1865.	Civil War begins.	*Gone with the Wind* starring Clark Gable and Vivien Leigh *Shenandoah* starring Jimmy Stewart.	GONE WITH THE WIND by Margaret Mitchell and IN MY FATHER'S HOUSE by Ann Rinaldi	
1862	U.S. begins printing paper greenbacks to finance Civil War. By 1865 more than $400 million have been printed.				
1864		"In God We Trust" appears on a U.S. coin for the first time.			
1865	Depression begins, lasts till 1867. Greenback dollar worth 35 cents in gold.	Civil War ends.			*How Government Intervention Plagued Our 19th-Century Economy*, see page 44 of this book
1866	Congress authorizes the 5 cent coin, the nickel, minted of copper and nickel with not more than 25% nickel.	Civil Rights Act passed.			
1867		Alaska purchased from Russia for $7.2 million.			
1868		Fourteenth Amendment ratified. Congress passes bill regulating work day for federal employees to 8 hours.			

Year	U.S. Economic History	Other Historical Events	Movie tie-in	For Further Reading	For Further Study
1869	Congress enacts Public Credit Act, provides for payment of U.S. debts in gold. $356 million Greenback dollars are left in circulation. With passive assent of high officials in White House and Treasury, Jay Gould and James Fisk try to rig investment markets. Wall Street panics, "Black Friday" crash. Recession begins.	First U.S. transcontinental rail route completed. Congress adopts Fifteenth Amendment, states the right to vote shall not be denied due to "race, color or previous condition of servitude."			
1870	U.S. federal debt $2.4 billion.	Fifteenth Amendment ratified. U.S. population: 39.8 million (4.9 million are freed Negroes; 2.3 million are immigrants who have arrived since 1860).			
1873	Coinage Act of Congress makes gold the U.S. Monetary standard, eliminates all silver currency. Financial panic in New York, September, 1873. Depression begins, downturn lasts 65 months.				
1875	Congress passes Specie Resumption Act, provides for specie (coin) payments on January 1, 1879. Greenbacks in circulation are reduced from $382 million to $300 million.				
1877		Reconstruction era ends. Southern states regain control of their governments.			
1878	Bland-Allison Act mandates the Treasury's purchase of $2-4 million in silver bullion per month. Overvalues silver. Sets Gresham's Law into motion.				*How Government Intervention Plagued Our 19th-Century Economy*, see page 44 of this book
1879	U.S. resumes specie payment. Greenbacks are worth their face value in gold.				
1880	U.S. federal debt $2.1 billion.	U.S. population: 50.1 million			
1882	Recession begins.	Congress passes Chinese Exclusion Act: excludes Chinese laborers from entering U.S. for ten years.			
1885		Immigrants from eastern and southern Europe arrive (largely Jewish, escaping persecution from Russia).			

Year	U.S. Economic History	Other Historical Events	Movie tie-in	For Further Reading	For Further Study
1887	Recession begins.				
1889		Oklahoma (Indian Territory) Land Rush.			
1890	Recession begins. U.S. federal debt $1.1 billion. Five pounds of flour costs 14.5 cents. Ten pounds of potatoes, 16 cents. Sherman Silver Purchase Act requires Treasury to buy almost entire output of American silver mines and overvalues the silver; also issues new paper "Treasury Notes" redeemable in either silver or gold.				
1891	Foreigners begin withdrawing capital from U.S.				
1892		Chinese Exclusion Act extended for ten years.			
1893	Gold reserves fall below $90 million. Panic of 1893. Depression begins, downturn lasts 17 months. Sherman Silver Purchase Act of 1890 repealed.				
1894	Government sells bonds to replenish gold reserve. First graduated income tax law passed by Congress.				
1895	Recession begins, downturn lasts 18 months. Supreme Court declares income tax unconstitutional (Pollack v. Farmers Loan and Trust Company).				
1896	Dow Jones Industrial Average (DJIA) first appears, May 26, 1896.				
1897	National Monetary Conference endorses existing gold standard.				
1898		Spanish-American War begins and ends.			
1899	Recession begins.				
1900	U.S. federal debt $1.3 billion. Congress enacts Gold Standard Act, making other forms of money redeemable in gold.	U.S. population: 75.9 million. Life expectancy: 48 years for females; 51 years for males.			
circa 1901	U.S. conquest of Philippines kills 220,000 Philippinos. Start of U.S. Empire.				
1902		Chinese Exclusion Act extended.			

Year	U.S. Economic History	Other Historical Events	Movie tie-in	For Further Reading	For Further Study
1906	DJIA closes above 100 for the first time.				
1907	Panic of 1907. Many banks fail. Depression begins.			*Little Britches* series by Ralph Moody	
1909		Lincoln penny replaces Indian Head penny.			
1910	Recession begins. U.S. federal debt $1.1 billion. Yield on 50-year corporate bonds, 3.8%.	U.S. population: 91.9 million			
1913	Federal income tax created through 16th Amendment. Until now, federal government was small enough to get along on customs duties and liquor and tobacco taxes. Federal Reserve System created to control quantity of money in U.S. Money supply is $11 billion. Five pounds of flour costs 16.5 cents.	British pound still backed by gold and silver. Prices in Britain still average same as in 1661. U.S. senators now elected directly by voters, not states.			
1914	Federal Trade Commission established. Gold: $20.67, silver: $0.50, platinum: $45.14 U.S. money supply: $11.6 billion.	World War I begins.		WORLD WAR I by Richard Maybury, published by Bluestocking Press	
1918		World War I ends.			
1919		Eighteenth Amendment ratified. Prohibits the manufacture, sale, import, or export of liquor in the U.S.			
1920	Money supply is $23.7 billion. Depression begins, lasts till 1921. U.S. federal debt $24.3 billion. Yield on 50-year corporate bonds is 5.1%.	Nineteenth Amendment gives women the right to vote.			
1921	Money supply is down to $20.7 billion. Federal Reserve begins inflating to end the depression. The money goes not into consumer items but into stocks. Consumer prices rise little but stock prices begin a long climb. Feelings of prosperity help create the "Roaring Twenties."				
1926	Five pounds of flour costs 30 cents.				
1927		"Black Friday" in Germany. German economic system collapses.			

Year	U.S. Economic History	Other Historical Events	Movie tie-in	For Further Reading	For Further Study
1929	Money supply has risen to $26.2 billion. Stock investors are euphoric. Federal Reserve stops inflating money supply. In October, the "Great Stock Market Crash." DJIA plummets 38.33 points on October 28, 1929. Great Depression begins, lasts till 1941.				
1930	U.S. federal debt $16.2 billion.	U.S. population: 122.7 million; Life expectancy: 61 years			
1933	Gold backing of U.S. dollar removed for domestic transactions; retained for foreign transactions. Americans forbidden to own gold. Five pounds of flour costs 19.5 cents.	Franklin Roosevelt's New Deal legislation begins delivering coup de grace to common law; power of Federal government expanded enormously. 21st Amendment repeals prohibition.			
1935		Social Security Act enacted.			
1936	Money supply expanding, depression reduced.				
1937	Money supply expansion slows, depression worsens.				
1940	U.S. federal debt $43 billion. Money supply $38.7 billion. Five pounds of flour costs 21.5 cents.	U.S. population: 131.6 million			
1941	Massive expansion of money supply begins. July, 1941, Franklin Roosevelt cuts off Japanese oil supply. Great Depression ends.	December 7, 1941 Japanese attack Pearl Harbor.U.S. declares war on Japan, Germany, and Italy.		WORLD WAR II by Richard Maybury, published by Bluestocking Press	
1944	Bretton Woods Agreement tied currency exchange rates to U.S. dollar and tied U.S. dollar to gold at the rate of $35 U.S. dollars per ounce of gold. Int'l Monetary Fund also established.				
1945	Recession begins. Money supply $94.1 billion. Five pounds of flour costs 32.1 cents; 10 pounds of potatoes costs 49.3 cents. UN "World Bank" founded.	World War II ends. Nuremburg Trials. United Nations Charter signed.	*Judgment at Nuremberg* starring Spencer Tracy		
1948	Recession begins.				
1950	U.S. federal debt $257.4 billion.	Korean War. U.S. population: 150.6 million			

Year	U.S. Economic History	Other Historical Events	Movie tie-in	For Further Reading	For Further Study
1953	Recession begins.				
1955	Five pounds of flour costs 53.8 cents.				
1956	DJIA closes above 500 for the first time on March 12, 1956.				
1957	Recession begins.				
1959	First U.S. combat deaths in Vietnam triggered big inflations of 1970s (federal government printed money to finance war and raised taxes).				
1960	Recession begins. U.S. federal debt $284.1 billion.	U.S. population: 179.3 million			
1965	Silver removed from U.S. dimes and quarters. Reduced to 40% for half dollars.	President Johnson orders air raids on North Vietnam and sends U.S. troops. Medicare established.		VIETNAM: A HISTORY by Stanley Karnow published by Penguin.	
1965-70	Coin shortage. Americans hoard silver coins.				
1969	Recession begins. Silver removed from all U.S. coinage.				
1970	U.S. federal debt $370.1 billion.	U.S. population: 205 million			
1971	All gold backing removed from U.S. dollar. Nixon imposes 90-day freeze on wages, prices, and rents.	26th Amendment ratified, lowering voting age from 21 to 18.			For research: determine if, as of the 1970s , all governments have issued fiat currencies that can be created without limit.
1972	DJIA closes above 1000 for the first time November 14, 1972.				
1973	Recession begins.	U.S. population: 210 million. U.S. discontinues combat operations in Vietnam.			
1974	Wage and price controls end.				
1975		Vietnam War ends.			
1980	Recession begins. U.S. federal debt $908 billion. U.S. money supply $412 billion. Yields on 30-year corporate bonds, 13%. (50-year bonds no longer exist.)	U.S. population: 226,550,000			
1981	Recession begins.				
1982	Worst recession since Great Depression. DJIA is 777. Federal Reserve begins rapid inflation of money supply. Money goes into stocks.				

Year	U.S. Economic History	Other Historical Events	Movie tie-in	For Further Reading	For Further Study
1986	Federal debt passes $2 trillion mark, having doubled in 5 years.				
1987	DJIA closes above 2000 for the first time on January 8, 1987. Federal Reserve slows inflation of money supply. October 19, 1987 the index falls 508 points, a record drop of 22.6%, the biggest one-day drop in its history. Known as the Black Monday crash. Inflation of money supply is quickly resumed.				*Nine Myths About the Crash* by Murray N. Rothbard, page 71 of this book.
1988	Five pounds of flour costs $1.08. Ten pounds of potatoes, $2.88.				
1989	U.S. middle class is 63.3% of population, down from 71.2% in 1969. Poor: 14.7%, up from 10.9%.	Berlin Wall falls. Breakup of Soviet empire begins.			
1990	Inflation of money supply is slowed. Recession begins. DJIA hits 3000 on July 13, 1990, then drops sharply. Oil hits $40 per barrel. U.S. federal debt $3.23 trillion.	Iraq-Kuwait war begins.		THE THOUSAND YEAR WAR IN THE MIDEAST by Richard Maybury, published by Bluestocking Press	
1991	Average non-supervisory worker earns $7.46 (in 1982 dollars), a 13% drop from $8.55 in 1973. Taxes are higher than in 1973. Money supply is $950 billion. Inflation of money supply is resumed. Recession ends. In a repeat of the 1920s, the newly created money goes not into consumer prices but stock prices, leading to the Roaring Nineties. DJIA closes above 3000 for the first time on April 17, 1991.	U.S. declares victory, withdraws from Iraq.			
1992	U.S. dollar worth only 13 cents of 1945 value; 10 cents of 1933; 7.5 cents of 1913; 6 cents of 1900. U.S. federal debt $4 trillion (estimated). In recent years, people have been shifting the way they hold money, causing the old benchmark measure of money supply, M1, to deflate as M2 inflates dramatically. M2 is $3.4 trillion. The DJIA hits 3794.				

Year	U.S. Economic History	Other Historical Events	Movie tie-in	For Further Reading	For Further Study
1995	DJIA closes above 4,000 for the first time on February 23, 1995. DJIA closes above 5,000 for the first time on November 21, 1995.				
1996	M2 is $3.8 trillion. DJIA closes above 6,000 for the first time on October 14, 1996.				
1997	In February, M2 hits $3.9 trillion and the DJIA closes for the first time above 7,000 on February 17, 1997 (at 89 trading days, fastest 1,000-point gain to date); in June DJIA closes at 7700. July 16, 1997 DJIA closes above 8,000 for the first time. Unemployment is down to 5%. In the stock market, the Roaring Nineties have surpassed the Roaring Twenties, stocks are more expensive than at any other time in history including the 1920s. Federal debt surpasses $5.3 trillion. U.S. military combat strength has been cut to half that of 1990. Iran and Iraq have been strengthening their military forces; Iran has fortified the Strait of Hormuz. 65% of total world oil deposits are in the Persian Gulf.				
1998	Federal debt as of April, 1998: $5.5 trillion dollars. DJIA closes above 9,000 points in April 1998.	U.S. population: 269,381,853			
1999	March 29, 1999 the DJIA closes above 10,000 points for the first time. May 3, 1999 closes above 11,000 points for the first time. It took the Dow just over a month to reach 11,000, the fastest 1,000 point jump to date.				

Year	U.S. Economic History	Other Historical Events	Movie tie-in	For Further Reading	For Further Study
March 2000	Federal debt as of March 2000: $5.7 trillion dollars, specifically: $5,726,473,086,205. The federal debt is increasing an average of $220 million per day since March 31, 1999.	U.S. population: 274,863,130			
2001	By 2001 the 1990s stock market boom is over. Stock crash nearly identical replay of 1929. 2001 recession begins.				
Sept. 11, 2001	On September 11, 2001, in an attack against the United States, over 3000 civilians were murdered. The World Trade Center in New York was destroyed, as well as a portion of the Pentagon. Four civilian airliners were destroyed, including passengers and crew. This attack is also referred to as Sept. 11, Sept. 11 Attack, and 9-11. Just before Sept. 11 gold was $271, silver was $4.18, platinum was $443			THE THOUSAND YEAR WAR IN THE MIDEAST by Richard Maybury, published by Bluestocking Press	
September 2004	Federal debt as of Sept. 2004: $7.3 trillion dollars, specifically: $7,380,494,657,749. The federal debt has continued to increase an average of $1.69 billion per day since Sept. 30, 2003.	U.S. population: 294,307,056			
mid 2006	U.S. housing market peaks.				
February 27, 2007	DJIA loses 416 points, its biggest one-day point loss since Sept. 17, 2001 when the 30-share index tumbled nearly 685 points.				
mid-2007	First inflationary burst in the Great Economic Crisis begins, lasting until June 2008; people flee from U.S. dollar, velocity rises; subprime mortgage industry collapses.				Research the monetary crisis of the Zimbabwean dollar. Search online "Zimbabwean dollar".

Year	U.S. Economic History	Other Historical Events	Movie tie-in	For Further Reading	For Further Study
February 27, 2007	DJIA peaks at 14,164.				
January 24, 2008	Nat'l Assoc. of Realtors releases data showing largest single year drop in U.S.home sales in 25 years.				
mid-2008	Deflationary burst as subprime mortgage disaster breaks loose, people flee back into the dollar, velocity falls. Credit crunch.				
March 2009	U.S. stock market drops to its lowest level in 12 years, just over 6500 March 6, 2009.				
January 27, 2009	Iceland's government collapses.				
February 17, 2009	U.S. President Barack Obama signs $787 billion stimulus package into law.				
August 2009	Gold, $938, silver $13.43, platinum $1175.				
2010		U.S. population: 308.4 million projected, pending completion of the U.S. census			
March 23, 2010	U.S. President Barack Obama signs Patient Protection and Affordable Care Act into law.				
September 2010	Federal Debt: $13,423,505,000, 000 ($43,276 per taxpayer). See usdebtclock.org for current statistics. DJIA 10,447 Gold $1247, silver $19.84, platinum $1555.				
				Compare free market analysis to mainstream media reporting (with parental permission and oversight). Peruse *Reference Sources* and *Web sites of Interest* on pages 97 and 98 of this student study guide.	Bring the following data current: What is M2 today? What is the Dow Jones Industrial Average today? What is the current rate of unemployment? What is the federal debt? To find the current federal debt, conduct a web search for "U.S. federal debt".

Published by Bluestocking Press

Uncle Eric Books by Richard J. Maybury

UNCLE ERIC TALKS ABOUT PERSONAL, CAREER, AND FINANCIAL SECURITY

WHATEVER HAPPENED TO PENNY CANDY?

WHATEVER HAPPENED TO JUSTICE?

ARE YOU LIBERAL? CONSERVATIVE? OR CONFUSED?

ANCIENT ROME: HOW IT AFFECTS YOU TODAY

EVALUATING BOOKS: WHAT WOULD THOMAS JEFFERSON THINK ABOUT THIS?

THE MONEY MYSTERY

THE CLIPPER SHIP STRATEGY

THE THOUSAND YEAR WAR IN THE MIDEAST

WORLD WAR I: THE REST OF THE STORY

WORLD WAR II: THE REST OF THE STORY

Bluestocking Guides (student study guides for the Uncle Eric books)
written by: either Jane A. Williams, Kathryn Daniels, or Ann Williams

A BLUESTOCKING GUIDE: BUILDING A PERSONAL MODEL FOR SUCCESS

A BLUESTOCKING GUIDE: ECONOMICS (based on WHATEVER HAPPENED TO PENNY CANDY?)

A BLUESTOCKING GUIDE: JUSTICE (based on WHATEVER HAPPENED TO JUSTICE?)

A BLUESTOCKING GUIDE: POLITICAL PHILOSOPHIES (based on ARE YOU LIBERAL? CONSERVATIVE? OR CONFUSED?)

A BLUESTOCKING GUIDE: ANCIENT ROME (based on ANCIENT ROME: HOW IT AFFECTS YOU TODAY)

A BLUESTOCKING GUIDE: SOLVING THE MONEY MYSTERY (based on THE MONEY MYSTERY)

A BLUESTOCKING GUIDE: APPLYING THE CLIPPER SHIP STRATEGY (based on THE CLIPPER SHIP STRATEGY)

A BLUESTOCKING GUIDE: THE THOUSAND YEAR WAR IN THE MIDEAST [PDF download]

A BLUESTOCKING GUIDE: WORLD WAR I: THE REST OF THE STORY

A BLUESTOCKING GUIDE: WORLD WAR II: THE REST OF THE STORY

Each Study Guide includes some or all of the following:
   1) chapter-by-chapter comprehension questions and answers
   2) application questions and answers
   3) research activities
   4) essay assignments
   5) thought questions
   6) final exam

More Titles Published by Bluestocking Press

LAURA INGALLS WILDER AND ROSE WILDER LANE HISTORICAL TIMETABLE

ECONOMICS: A FREE MARKET READER edited by Jane Williams & Kathryn Daniels

CAPITALISM FOR KIDS: GROWING UP TO BE YOUR OWN BOSS by Karl Hess

COMMON SENSE BUSINESS FOR KIDS by Kathryn Daniels

The Young Thinker's Bookshelf

Visit Bluestocking Press's online store at www.BluestockingPress.com for more information or contact Bluestocking Press at: customerservice@bluestockingpress.com for details.

To order any of the above items, visit Bluestocking Press online for selection and order information.

Bluestocking Press
Phone: 800-959-8586
Questions: CustomerService@BluestockingPress.com
web site: www.BluestockingPress.com